<u>DEDICATION</u>

Special thanks to my dear friends Pastor Bob and Peggy Duff, my wife Kim Pike, Alice Pike, Jessica Mitchell, Charlie Wolfinger, Randy Thornton, my Aunt Dona Morrow and Dean and Karen Bosler.

To My Parents Charles and Virginia Pike.

Also, thanks to my Cardiologist Doctor Chaudhry, my VAD nurse Kelly Terry, and all the Doctors and Nurses at St. Vincent Hospital Indianapolis and a special thank you to the thousands of people who prayed for me around the clock while I was in the hospital for a month.

In Memory of

Odie R. Carrier Jr.　　　(1953 -2018)

Vic Withers Jr., 70, COVID (1950-2020)

Steven Hawkins, 66, COVID (1954 -2021)

Chris Haycraft, 58, COVID (1963 - 2021)

Introduction

I would like to start out by saying I am no one special. I am a believer in Jesus Christ, but I am a sinner. I make no claims that I am perfect because I know I am *far* from it. But for some reason in 2019, while in a coma for two days, I was given a glimpse of heaven and hell.

It may be contradictory to what others have experienced and it may even be different than the Bible itself. What you are about to read is what I witnessed; I was told to take note of it.

I did not have any measuring devices, but I was told to take note of all I saw and heard. Somehow, I just knew these numbers and information as if someone was telling me or uploaded it into my memory.

I was only in heaven and hell for what seemed to be a noticeably short time. But since time in heaven is irrelevant to what we determine as time here on earth I have no way of knowing how long I was there. I am sure there is much more to Heaven and Hell than what I saw. But I was told to go back and tell anyone and everyone what I witnessed.

Anyone that knows me knows that I am a proud follower of Christ. But I must admit I have never read the bible cover to cover. I do not claim to know everything in it, and I cannot quote chapter and verse like many of my friends.

That doesn't mean I don't have a close relationship with my Lord Jesus. He has been in my life since I was very young, and I see how God works. Look around throughout the day and notice God working in your life. He is everywhere, in everything, and He is answering prayers all the time. We just need to seek Him and understand that things happen in God's timing not ours no matter how hard we push it. You don't have to know the bible inside and out to have a relationship with our God, but it helps you to understand Him better.

I have heard a few excerpts in church about the book of Revelations, but I have personally never read Revelations.

I have been told by several people that my story resembles what is told in the book of Revelations concerning New Jerusalem. However, I will not read Revelations or discuss it with anyone until after I finish my book. I don't want it to influence my story. I want to give you my story as I witnessed it, just as I was told to do.

I have also been told by others that there are books out there talking about other people's experience with heaven or hell, but I have never read any of them nor heard about them. I have no idea how any of those stories compare to my experience, nor will I read them until after my book is finished. I know that people out there will deny my story as truth. In fact, I was told by Jesus himself that I would be persecuted for telling my story. But when the Lord tells you to go and tell what you have seen, you do it.

Before I get to what I witnessed, I would like to tell you a little about what I went through in my life and some of the things that led up to this experience.

In My Youth:

I came to know the Lord Jesus Christ as a child of only six years of age while attending Washington Avenue Baptist Church in Evansville, Indiana. Brother Clayman was the pastor at the time.

I will never forget that moment. In front of my mother and father I joyfully accepted Jesus in my heart. I stood in front of the congregation as each member lined up, walked by, and shook my hand. I tried to be a big man, but I must admit that I was overcome with emotion and cried like a baby.

Looking back on my life, I now know that I have had heart problems from an early age. Heart problems run in both sides of my family. I do not remember exactly how old I was when my heart started to give me problems, but I do remember as a child of five playing with my friends outside and my heart would start jumping (*I know now it was misfiring and skipping beats*). As a child I could only describe it as two raccoons were fighting under my shirt. I cannot say that it really hurt. It was more frustrating than anything.

One summer afternoon I felt my "raccoons" and I was aggravated. So, I made a fist and I hit myself in the chest as hard as I could. My heart started beating normal again. From that point on that's how I would correct my heart when I felt the "raccoons fighting." Then I would run and catch up with my best friend Odie Carrier and my other friends. I just wanted to run and play.

My fist pounding method worked for years. I did not even think to tell my parents about it until I was in my 20s.

Keep in mind that this was the 1960s. People did not talk about heart problems much. The knowledge of the heart was nothing like today's technology.

For example, in 1962 my great uncle, Bernard Pike, had been feeling weak and had a pain in his chest so he went to his doctor. He was told that he just had simple heart burn. Bernard left the doctor's office. On the way home Bernard had a massive heart attack and died while driving. His car slammed into a light pole, and they said he was gone before impact. Today he would have been sent in for a multitude of tests, not just sent home. It is truly amazing how far our medical technology has advanced in the last 60 years.

My Father's Experience:

Most people who know me and my family also know that when I was just a boy of ten, my father had a similar experience to mine. I am including it so you can compare for yourself. Although it is similar in some ways, he did not experience the things I was told to tell you. My dad only witnessed Heaven, he never mentioned anything about Hell.

It was a hot and sunny Saturday in July 1967. I was ten years old at the time and had been out playing with my friends. When I walked in the back door of the kitchen at lunchtime, my mother asked me to go out and get my father for lunch. My mother was in the kitchen preparing the food as she always did. She would always cook enough for friends if they happened to show up, but that day it was just the three of us.

6

There was a sixty-foot-long sidewalk that ran from our back patio to our driveway and the garage. Between the house and the garage there was a row of about twelve exceptionally large pine trees. They were incredibly old, very green, and healthy pine trees that had grown together. They were so thick that you could not see between them. They almost formed a wall.

Behind the pine trees was a ten-foot opening from the trees to the garage's outer wall. We placed our trash cans against that wall so they could not be seen from the house. Twenty feet to the left of the trash cans was our well. The well was easily seen past the pine trees but could not be seen from the house.

Thinking my dad was in the garage, I was headed that way to get him for lunch. As I walked past the ten-foot opening between the pine trees and the garage I looked to my left and saw my dad laying on the ground next to the well. My father was in his white T shirt, old work pants and shoes, the ones he always wore while relaxing around the house or working in the yard.

I thought he was laying down working on something or just relaxing in the shade from working, so I yelled "Dad, lunch is ready." But he did not respond. Thinking he just didn't hear me or was joking around, I walked over to where he was laying and took my foot and jokingly kicked the bottom of his shoe to get his attention. Once again, I said "Hey Dad, lunch is ready. Mom said to come in and eat." But he still didn't move.

At that moment, I felt something was wrong. I could see he was lying on his side, facing downward. He was not moving or responding to my voice.

Apparently dad decided he was going to work on the well by himself but did not tell anyone. The old well in our yard had a heavy 80lb concrete slab for a lid with a metal handle made from rebar. We now know he had been pulling and tugging to lift the lid cover by himself and fell to the ground unconscious.

When I found him, he was face down and not moving. I knelt and with my hand I rolled him over onto his back. I noticed immediately that he felt cold to the touch. He was not breathing, and his lips were blue. In a panicked voice I yelled as loud as I could for my mom.

Mom immediately dropped what she was doing and ran out to me. Once she saw dad lying on the ground lifeless, mom ran back to the house as fast as she could and called the local fire department. She then ran back to us. Mom raised dad into her arms and held him until the firemen showed up.

Remember, this was during the 60s and not only were there no cell phones but at that time there was no such thing as a 911 emergency number. You called the local fire department or dialed "0" and the operator would connect you to the nearest fire station.

When the firemen arrived, mom gently laid dad back down and moved out of the way. The firemen, or EMT's as we call them today, began trying to resuscitate him. In the 60s, CPR was very primitive compared to today's standards, but they did all they knew to do at the time.

So much time had passed that they did not seem to think he would make it.

The firemen were all knelt around him and shaking their heads as if to indicate that my dad was gone. It was then I heard one of the men say, "I cannot get a pulse." The firemen slowly began to rise to their feet. At that very moment, we heard dad gasp for air. The sound was so loud that it took everyone by surprise. Dad immediately sat up and took a very deep and long breath. I heard my dad yelling, "I don't want to go back! I want to stay here! Please, please! I don't want to be there anymore I want to stay, please!"

The firemen immediately made him lie back down and the EMTs began checking his vitals again. After making sure he was stable, they rushed him to the hospital in the ambulance.

They would not let us ride with him in the ambulance and mom did not drive. So, mom called a taxi for the two of us. We prayed in the taxi the whole way to the hospital. We prayed for God to make dad whole again. When we arrived at the hospital, we ran to the registration desk. They told us to have a seat and the doctor would be out to talk to us after they finished examining him.

One of the firemen that had been on the scene and worked on dad came up to us in the hospital emergency waiting room. He said he had never seen anything like that in his 15 years of service. He told us that by all rights, dad should not be there. The fireman then told us that dad was now sitting up in the bed and talking like nothing had even happened and was asking when he could go home.

Mother and I prayed for hours nonstop in the waiting room. We found out that the doctors had been observing him and running tests. The doctors determined that there was no damage of any kind. They were astounded and said they had never seen anything like it. They finally released my father from the hospital with a clean bill of health. My mother used a payphone and called a cab so we could return home. After returning home, Dad rested over the weekend and went back to work on Monday as if nothing had ever happened.

It's important to note that the fire station was at least 20 minutes away from our house. And we do not know how long dad had been laying there before we found him. If the oxygen supply is interrupted to the brain, consciousness will be lost within fifteen seconds and damage to the brain begins to occur after about four minutes without oxygen. A complete interruption of oxygen to the brain is referred to as cerebral anoxia. A full recovery from severe anoxic or hypoxic brain injury is rare, even today.

At the time, I did not think much about it because I was happy to see dad alive again. But *God* was at work for sure. By all reason, my dad should have had some sort of brain damage, but there was none.

Several years had passed and we hardly spoke of the incident anymore. Then one evening, while sitting on the back patio, as we did almost every summer evening, my dad asked my mother and I if we would sit down for just a minute and listen to him. He said that he wanted to tell us about something that had happened to him.

Our family was very open about things, and since I was an only child, my mother and father were my best friends. I enjoyed sitting around and talking with them. We always talked about our day and what went on every evening at the dinner table or later while sitting on the patio. We were waiting for him to tell us about something that happened at work that day as he usually did.

I remember dad looking a little uncomfortable as he started to tell us his story. He leaned forward, folded his hands, and placed them under his chin with his elbows on his knees. He stared at the ground between his legs took a deep breath and slowly exhaled before he continued. "I need to tell you both something. You are probably going to think I am crazy, but I can't keep this to myself any longer."

He looked nervous and uneasy, but he continued. "When you found me laying by the well several years ago, something happened to me that I have never talked about. But I must tell someone."

It seemed strange to know that my dad had kept something secret especially for that length of time. I listened as he took a deep breath and continued, "Well I need to tell you both about what happened that day. I will never forget it."

He paused and took another deep breath, "While straining to lift the lid I felt a horrific pain in my chest. I grabbed my chest with my hand and gasped for breath but I fell to the ground. Then nothing. Everything went black. Then I saw a light above me in the distance and felt as though I was lifted or tugged toward the light. I felt like I was floating weightlessly. I felt a second tug and stopped about fifteen or twenty feet in the air horizontally, face down towards earth. I looked down and could see you both bending over a body laying by the well, but I was confused." He looked at mother and said, "I saw you lift my head up into your lap and hug me. You both were crying very hard. I realized the person on the ground you were holding was me."

I could hear my mother's breath quicken as she recalled the heartache of that moment. Then dad told us "I remember thinking how can this be? I am here. I yelled out 'I am up here! Look up!' I heard you both crying but you kept looking down at my body. I felt a third tug and went up another fifty feet or so into the air. Everyone became smaller and less significant the farther up I went. I could see the ambulance and the firefighters gathering around me. At that moment I could not see or hear you or anything else down here on earth."

He continued looking confused and almost afraid, "I felt a fourth tug, and all around me I saw these creatures that seemed to be dressed like monks. They had on what appeared to be brown or dark colored robes with something tied around their waists. As they scurried towards me, I was tugged up again a fifth time before they could get to me. They were reaching for me trying to grab at me. As I ascended higher, they were looking up at me."

Dad paused here as his emotions overwhelmed him to the point he could hardly speak, he cleared his throat and then he continued, "I know this is hard to believe, but their faces appeared to be skeletons. And even though there was no flesh on their faces I could see disappointment in their demeanor as if they had failed somehow. After the fifth tug I stood upright."

My dad paused again to gather his thoughts. Until that point, he had looked away from us the entire time. He took a deep breath and sighed and with tears streaming down both of his cheeks he looked right at us as he continued to speak and tell us his experience.

Dad reached out and took both my hand and mother's hand and leaned toward us. With an extremely serious look he pulled us closer to him and said with a quivering soft voice, "The light that took me there surrounded me completely. I felt a love that I cannot describe." He paused, took a deep breath and then continued, "As it engulfed me, I felt like I became a part of it. When I turned around, the bright light was getting larger and more defined and all I wanted to do was to go deeper into the light, it was incredible."

He became very emotional again, so much so that his voice was quivering to the point we could not understand him. He broke down and wept like a man that lost everything he held dear. He had to pause to regain his composure. "I walked into the warm bright light and felt as though it was calling to me." Again, he paused then continued, "And that is when I saw heaven. It was the most beautiful place I have ever seen". He said this with such conviction that we could not doubt him.

"But a voice told me, 'For you Charles, it is not yet time. You must go back.' Then I felt like I was falling backward from heaven at an incredible speed. I was yelling desperately at the voice, 'I don't want to go back. *Please* do not send me back, I do not want to be there anymore. I want to stay here! Please!' The next thing I knew I opened my eyes. There were several men around me, and one yelled that he found my pulse. They began working franticly on me. I was trying to get up, but they held me down and kept telling me to take it easy.'"

Dad continued in a more calm, almost disappointed tone, "Then they rolled me onto a board and lifted me up and strapped me onto a gurney. They moved me to the ambulance and took me to the hospital with sirens squealing as fast as they could go. I kept telling them I was fine. I felt fine, but I did not say anything about what happened to me."

I remember being in awe of Dad's story. My dad was in heaven; he had seen it and came back. We could tell by the way he told the story that he was not making it up. He told his story to many people over the years, but never once did it change. He never added to it, and he never left anything out. We knew that my father, Charles Pike, had experienced heaven.

After his experience in heaven, things changed for my dad and our family. His business grew and expanded far beyond what we thought was possible for our small family business. All aspects of business just seemed to flow effortlessly. Dad seemed to connect with everyone almost immediately. No one ever seemed to be a stranger to him. I always felt like my dad was so successful in his life, not just financially, but in so many ways because of his experience.

One example of his unique success was that although we lived in the state of Indiana, my father was given the honorary title of Kentucky Colonel. The commission of Kentucky Colonel is the highest title of honor bestowed by the Governor of Kentucky. It is recognition of an individual's noteworthy accomplishments and outstanding service to the Kentucky community, state, and nation. If you are a commissioned Colonel, you are a Kentucky Colonel for life.

I felt because he touched holy ground everyone seemed to love him and go to him for advice. Family, friends, and even people he did not know would come up to him on the street and ask him for advice as if they knew him.

One example was when a tall, fifty-something, well-dressed man with graying hair came into our factory one day and asked if Charlie was around. He was hoping to speak with him again. When we informed the gentleman that dad had gone to be with the Lord a few years prior, the man turned away as to not face us and broke down and started weeping.

It took him a while to compose himself. After a few minutes he looked back at us and apologized for crying. I told him that I understood. Then he looked at me and asked if I was Charlie's son. I nodded and smiled as the family resemblance was undeniable.

The man went on to say "You may not know this, but your dad and I grew close when I was just a kid around 10 years old. I was walking home from school one day and it

15

had started pouring down rain. Not just a normal rain but a real heavy downpour that caused the water to back up over the sidewalk. I stepped into the doorway of the building to get out of the rain. I did not even know what the building was. I was just a kid trying to keep from getting soaked." He said with a sad chuckle.

He continued "I was watching for the rain to subside when Charlie called me. I was only a kid and was expecting him to yell at me for trespassing. I almost ran back into the rain, but I am so glad I didn't. I found that Charlie was different than most adults I had encountered in my life. He was kind to me. He told me to come on in and brought me a towel to dry off. He offered me something to drink while I waited. We talked and he listened to me."

He shifted in his chair as if to explain in greater detail. "You know most adults will just ignore kids. But Charlie was genuinely interested in what I was saying. Eventually the rain died down, I thanked him, and returned to my walk home. But after that I would frequently stop in and visit Charlie for a quick chat. Years passed and I became an adult, but I never forgot Charlie. Every now and again I would stop in to say hello and every time he was genuinely happy to see me. He would always take time out of his busy day to listen to me. No one ever listened to me like he did. It shaped a big part of who I am today." He said with a proud smile.

I could tell that the man was truly impacted by his interactions with my dad. But it was just a confirmation to me of how amazing of man my dad really was and how blessed I was to have him as my dad.

The man sighed before continuing "As a child I was always told by the people around me that I was no good, stupid and would never amount to anything, but Charlie instilled in me that I could be anything and do anything I wanted if I applied myself. He informed me that he only went to school to the 8th grade, and he was a business owner because he never gave up on himself. And I will always be incredibly grateful to him for his kindness, caring and sincerity. Charlie is the reason I am the man I am today and because of him, I try to be like him and listen when kids need to talk.

There are many stories like this one that I have been told over the years. I could write a book on just the things people shared with me about my dad and mom helping them. Maybe I will, after this one.

One of the reasons I believed dad's story about his experience was that it never changed. Typically, when people make up a story it will vary a little here and there over time. But dad's story never faltered. While dad's story never changed there were things that he saw or experienced in heaven that he would not tell me. When I would ask what Heaven looked like, he would always respond, "Son there is nothing on this earth that I could even begin to compare the beauty to or even come close to explain it."

A businessman named Ken Langley walked into the factory one day and asked to talk to Charlie. I don't remember why he asked for dad specifically, but they became friends instantly. Later, we found out that Ken also had a similar experience seeing heaven. After that, when Ken visited, he and dad would talk about their experience in heaven. But at some point during their conversations, dad would ask me to leave and close the office door.

I was very hurt when he asked me to leave. Dad never excluded me from any conversation. So, one day I asked about it. Dad said "Son there are some things that Ken and I can discuss because we were both there. Things that we were told not to discuss with others. I am sorry, but I just cannot discuss certain things with you because I am not allowed to." I came to understand that dad witnessed things in heaven that he was bound to keep from anyone that had not already experience it.

Many years later, when we were talking about his experience in heaven, I remember saying to him that he was lucky. He *knew* it was real. The rest of us run on faith. People say they know that heaven is real, that they have studied or gone to church or listened to their parents tell them about it, so it must be real, but we are truly running on faith. Just because everyone believes something doesn't make it true. For example, people were told the earth was flat for hundreds of years. There were maps and drawings made to prove it. They believed this because they are taught this and told this repeatedly. It wasn't until someone traveled the world and witnessed firsthand that the world was round that we knew the truth. They believed this until they saw it for themselves and then they knew the truth for certain. We believe in heaven, but we run on faith until we see it and know it is true.

I want to pause for a moment here. Many people will shrug off my story now because they think it is a version of the story that my dad told me about his experience. I am not going to say that it does not resemble his story. My dad never mentioned Hell. He never said he saw or spoke to Jesus or anyone. He also did not speak of his experience in heaven for years because he was afraid people would think he was crazy. But I was told to take note of all I bore witness too, and to share. And it is up to you to decide what to believe. But if you believe nothing else, believe this: heaven exists! I have seen it and experienced it. Hell exists! I have seen it and experienced it. And Jesus is the only way to Heaven.

Back to My Story.

I tried to live a good life but, in my teens, and early twenties, like most people I got into my fair share of trouble. Most of which took place once I learned to drive. In the 1970s muscle cars and street racing were super popular. I owned a 1970 GTO and although I didn't drink or do recreational drugs, I was addicted to the adrenaline rush you got from driving super-fast cars. That being said, my list of speeding tickets was taller than I was.

I attended church off and on through most of my life. While I always had a close bond with our Lord and Savior and prayed daily. I did not always have a physical church, but I was okay with that because I knew my faith is not derived from a building. We are the body of Christ and we, the believers, are the Church. The Church is not a building.

My walk with the Lord was like most Christians. Though life had its ups and downs, I never lost my faith in the

Lord. I knew that Jesus was my Savior. I knew that no matter what happened in my life that I had salvation through Jesus Christ.

Just because we are believers in Christ, does not mean we are exempt from hardship or heartache. I worked side by side with my parents at our mattress factory since I was six years old. And over the years we worked some long, hard hours. When your family owns the business, you are always there when someone does not show up. When you own a business, and a job needs to be done, you do it. My parents said many times to work as unto the Lord. After working two and sometimes three shifts, we had built our family business to be very successful.

As I think back on it now, I know that even though we were blessed and even though we worked hard, Satan can still knock you down. We built our business up to a territory of thirteen states and employed sixty-two full-time and fifteen part-time employees. We were turning out ten semi-trailers and twelve straight trucks of bedding a week. But at the peak of it all we had three large accounts fail to pay us and the accounts went out of business which in turn caused us to go out of business. They were very large accounts.

The loss our company sustained from losing what those accounts owed us was impossible to recover. So, after years of trying to recover, we closed our wholesale manufacturing company. Because of bad advice from their attorney, my parents never incorporated. This meant they were a partnership so they were personally responsible for millions of dollars of company debt. which forced them to file personal bankruptcy too. When the company went under it dragged them with it. They lost their house, cars, jewelry, and everything else they owned. But they never once lost faith in God. They knew that He had a plan. And while Satan may have won the battle, our family won the war through the precious blood of Jesus.

While we had to close the wholesale business my wife Kim and I were able to open our own business shortly afterwards and manufacture and sell mattresses directly to the public. Mom and Dad always said "We lost a business, you started a business, but God's always been with us. We have never missed a meal and we still have a roof over our heads. And through the ups and downs in the coming years, we never lost our faith. Honestly, there were times when our faith was the only thing holding us up."

Kim and I both agreed before we were married that we did not want to have children. But we filled our hearts with fur-babies instead. Our first dog was a male Lhasa Apso named Big Mac. He was the closest to a child that anyone could have. I can still see the crooked smile he would give me when I took his picture. He was a photo hog. He was silly and loving and everything a fur-baby should be. He would "work" with me in the den late at night. While I was calculating costs and doing paperwork, he would lay under my desk and snore. I mention this because I saw him in Heaven, and yes there are animals in Heaven, I was so excited but more on that later.

A few years after we started our retail mattress store in 1992, we ran into Peggy Duff, a nice lady that worked at my chiropractor's office. When we mentioned that we needed the roof repaired on our home, Peggy introduced us to her husband Bob who was a contractor. And that began a lifelong friendship.

Because of Peggy and Bob's friendship Kim and I both grew considerably in our Christian walk. We became more involved and attended the church they went to. The church put on a very professional Easter and Christmas production directed by the minister of music Bob Tabor and his wife Ann. My friend Bob Duff built most of the set and invited Kim and I to help build the set. Later Kim volunteered to operate a stage light, and I ran a video camera and recorded the production. Those productions changed so many lives, including our own.

Over the next few years, Bob came to work with us at the mattress factory and retail store and we became like family. It was a few years before we realized that Bob's mom used to work for my dad when I was a small child. It is amazing to see God's plan. We like to think it shows God's sense of humor too.

After being in business for ten years our business had grown, and Kim was looking for some help in the office. So, in 2000 my dad suggested my cousin Alice who was attending high school at the time. Alice eagerly accepted and came to work for us. She was amazing at any task we threw at her. She took such an interest in the day-to-day workings of the business, learning each task of running the business as if it was her own. One day Kim and I were discussing Alice and how she was so dedicated to the business, especially for a young person at the time.

Since we had no children of our own and I was an only child, we didn't know who was going to carry on the business. Kim and I always figured we would sell the business off when we were ready to retire. But for some reason we felt that Alice might be interested in learning and one day owning and running the business. We asked her and she eagerly accepted.

Over the next 20 years we all grew closer to each other and to the Lord. We had corporate prayer every morning at work and all our employees were invited to join. We even had a few customers that joined in while we were having prayer. Alice's walk with the Lord became stronger through this and she would even lead in prayer. I am so proud of her and how strong her walk with Jesus has become.

Fast Forward to 2010

I was in a meeting in my office with Bob when I felt a pain in my chest. I tried to shrug it off like I usually did. But suddenly I felt like I was trapped in a bear hug. I asked Bob to tell the girls to call 9-1-1.

I had always joked that the men in our family usually had heart problems in their 50s. Well, sure enough I was in my 50s and after dozens of tests, I had been diagnosed with myocarditis. Basically, they think a virus had attacked my heart and weakened it. Unbeknownst to me at the time, this is what would lead to my experience. I was very upset at the time. I worked hard to stay in good shape. My job was very demanding and after getting off work I would stop at my dad's house and use his downstairs gym, work out with weights, then sit in the sauna and finish it off with at least 60 laps in the pool I did this at least 5 days a week. I had never drank alcohol, smoked or taken any type of recreational drugs in my life. The doctors said it was just luck of the draw, "nothing to beat yourself up over as you did not cause it."

Since my heart was weakened it was not able to pump the blood out efficiently and my heart had enlarged. The doctors said that the ejection fraction of my heart was 39%. We were shocked. But then the doctor explained that perfect health was between 60-70% so it was not as bad as it seemed, but it still was not good. I remember telling the doctors "But I feel fine. I do not have any chest pains. I can do anything that I could do before."

The doctors were amazed. One doctor said he had never seen a body adjust to a heart like my body had. I had none of the symptoms of heart failure. But several heart echoes and heart catheterization tests said otherwise. They wanted to put me on medication immediately.

The next problem we had was that I was allergic to the ace inhibitors they prescribed to treat my heart. Over the next few months doctors changed my medications so many times that we lost count. The medications they gave me were making basic tasks seemingly impossible. I would struggle to get up and get ready in the morning. I have always been an active person. So, sitting at my desk and being lethargic was no life for me.

God Healed My Heart:

I was at home sitting on the side of the bed one day and I prayed, "God, if you are going to heal me, please heal me now. If I am supposed to testify, then I will. Whatever your will is I will accept it." Suddenly out of nowhere I felt a warmth and a tingling on the top of my head. It felt like the palm of a hand coming down and laying across the top of my head.

Then the warmth and tingling spread down my head to my cheeks, to my neck, down my arms to my fingers. It continued to return up my arms and down both sides of my body. I felt the warmth spread down my legs to my toes and it returned up my body in the same manner. Then it felt like the hand was lifted off my head. I do not know how to explain it, but I knew in that moment that I was healed. I know many people will doubt it, but I immediately felt like myself again. The weakness, exhaustion, and weary feelings were all gone. I *knew* God had healed me.

I went downstairs and pulled our high-top custom conversion van out of the garage and started washing it. Kim ran out of the house yelling at me to stop. She knew I was not supposed to be exerting myself like that. I remember telling her, "God healed me!"

Then I explained how it happened. She looked a little hesitant at first, but she could tell by my face that I was different, so we stopped and thanked God.

A few days later we went to my doctor. He ordered the standard ECHO and heart-Cath tests again. Afterward he sat us down and said "I would like to say I had something to do with it, but I didn't. It is a miracle; it is all God. Your heart is back to normal size and is stronger. If anyone asks, I will tell them that God healed you. I'll even write a letter to your insurance company to tell them you are healed so you won't be on high-risk insurance anymore." He even took me off the medications and I was able to return to a normal life.

The doctor was astonished but being a believer, he could not doubt the miracle he saw. Just a few weeks ago he had told me that the only options I had was that the medications would help shrink my heart back down to normal or have a heart transplant. Now he was looking at the third option that he had forgotten about: God.

I told many people about God healing me. And to this day I will proudly proclaim that I received God's healing. But I learned something a year later, when you pray, be specific. I did not ask for God to heal me and never let it happen again. A year later I got sick again. But that never stopped me from proclaiming the miracle I had experienced. I was not upset about contracting myocarditis again. My God was capable of anything. I do not know why but I never prayed for healing like I did before. I just accepted that God wanted me to have this condition and moved on.

Next, we were back to the problem of me being allergic to the medications used to help my heart and was having a difficult time getting it regulated. After much prayer, we found a nurse practitioner that helped us get lined up on my medication a little better. She helped us to understand my problem in plain English. She broke the medical jargon down so we could understand it. You see, most people's heart problems derive from one of two areas, plumbing problems like clogged arteries or electrical; mine is electrical.

And for the next 10 years I was able to maintain a normal lifestyle with medication while having only 25% ejection fraction.

Economy Crash of 2008

After the economic crash in 2008, our business was struggling. Small independent businesses are usually hit hardest by disasters and ours was no exception. Not only was our business struggling but we lost my dad in 2009 and my mom in 2014. Alice had moved out of her apartment and into the house so we could save the money she was spending on rent. She moved into an apartment downstairs that my mom and dad lived in before they passed away. Satan had thrown every obstacle he could at us.

Most of my life had been trouble free but when the 2008 economic bubble popped, we were barely limping along. Then to make matters worse we lost my dad to cancer. I remember making the decision to have the life support terminated. It was one of the hardest decisions I've ever had to make. I remember being in his hospital room and holding his hand and as he drew his last breath. I looked at the ceiling and with tears in my eyes remembering what he had said about floating upwards from his body when he had his experience with Heaven and I said aloud, "Goodbye dad I will see you soon."

Going back a year before my dad had gotten sick, he called me into his office and said, "I want you to promise me something."

I responded "Of course."

Dad continued with a profoundly serious tone, "Please take care of your mother for me if I go to be with the Lord before her. Steve something is not right with your mother I can tell."

Shortly after dad had passed my mom started to suffer from dementia. Dad, being around her all the time, could tell that something was not right before she started showing symptoms, but he did not know how to explain it. We weren't around her like he was, so we did not see it until it became obvious.

As mother's dementia worsened, she would ask where dad was and when we told her he had passed she would re-live losing him all over again. We took care of mother and kept her home as long as we could, but, eventually, we had to place her in a nursing home. Keeping my promise to my dad we kept her home with us until 2012. She needed around-the-clock nursing care. So, we found a newly built nursing home that was equipped to care for her when it was no longer safe for us to do so at home. She was very well taken care of until she became sick and was taken to the hospital in 2014. While in the hospital she contracted pneumonia and once again, I had to make the decision to turn off the life support. The second hardest decision of my life.

In addition to trying to recover and regrow our struggling business we lost both my parents, as well as Kim's brother, mom, and dad. Leaving both of us with no immediate relatives. We lost more fur-babies than I care to list. We lost our last dog, Suzie in February 2019. This is the first time in a long time that we did not have any dogs.

Pause to talk about deciding on life support:

I want to pause here for a minute to say something to anyone who has ever had to make the decision or will have to make this decision in the future to turn off life support for a friend or loved one. The devil will try to make you feel guilty by making you wonder if you made the right decision. Do not let him win. Just make sure your friend or loved one is saved by the blood of Jesus and they will be in Heaven waiting for you when you arrive.

Part of the decline:

In 2011, a childhood friend of 44 years who worked for me at the time approached me one day and ask me if we had any work for his stepson as the boy had been laid off from work and needed money to help feed his family. We did not need any help, so I said no. The next day my friend's mother, Etta, called me and asked me the same thing and said it would be a favor to her if I could help the boy out in anyway. How do you say no to a woman that was like a second mother to you asking for a personal favor, plus I had known his stepson since the boy was about 8 years old.

We had some shelving we needed built and a few other small jobs. The boy was a contractor so as a favor to his grandmother I hired him as an independent contractor. He installed some insulation for us and repaired a fridge that wasn't running properly. He was to install the shelving for me on the second floor of our building as his next job. He did not work for us as an employee. He was hired as an independent contractor, so he was paid by the job, not by the hour.

One day he was on the second floor to take measurements for the shelving. He was told to let us know if he needed anything taken to the second floor that he could not carry up the stairway and we would have it brought up to him on our supply lift. We did not have an elevator, but our vertical reciprocating conveyor was used as a supply lift to move freight up and down our three-story building. It was not rideable by a person, but it moved freight that is too heavy or large to carry up the stairs.

To make a long story short, the man decided to walk out on the platform of this conveyor even though there was a large red and white sign warning against it and somehow it came crashing down to the first floor. We don't know why he was on the lift. And to this day we don't know how it came loose as none of the bolts or beams was broken.

The young man that I thought of as family surprised us by suing us, thus adding further to our hardships and an immense financial burden. While he was not an employee, he tried to sue us as one then when that didn't work sued us for negligence.

Most people that are not in business think that's what you have insurance for. But in truth insurance does not cover everything. We spent several hundred thousand dollars out of our pockets trying to settle this. And because of it we lost every type of insurance a business needs to operate. He even sued us personally and we even lost our homeowners and personal car insurance!

Satan knows how to kick you when you are down. And he was kicking us hard. It felt as though there was a black storm cloud hovering over us and was ready to break open at any moment.

As if all we were fighting wasn't enough, we had the breaks go out on a fork truck and damaged a main support beam in our building. And a storm pulled part of the roof off our building all within a year.

Because of the lawsuits we lost two of our businesses. We were forced to shut them down which cost us a massive loss of income and caused a lot of employee jobs to be lost as well. There were several investors in the two businesses all of whom lost large investments. The smallest being $20,000. The largest, including our own investment, was well over a net loss of $190,000 or more.

On top of our investment losses, we depleted all our savings due to the lawsuit. Then we had to start liquidating our assets just to keep our retail mattress factory in business. I was forced to sell my vintage 1970 GTO Judge, my mother's jewelry, and much more to pay attorney's fees, and to survive. To this day our employees have no idea how much we sacrificed to keep them employed. They have no idea how many meals we missed to keep food on their family's tables. Like I said before, when you are in business you are the one that must step up and do what needs to be done.

But through it all, we never lost our faith. We never said, "Why us, God?" Instead, we prayed every day and thanked God for what we were going though as we knew He could have changed any of it at any time, but there was a reason we were having to endure. We even prayed for the boy that was suing us and his family. God is always at work in your life. I laid it at the foot of the cross and walked away. We praised God and thanked Him for the difficult times as things will always get better. And we know God will always bring good things out of the bad things.

A very dear friend of ours, Dean Bosler, had commented that we were due for a break. He said he had never seen anyone hit or knocked down by so many obstacles and get back up repeatedly. Dean has been a friend for years and helped us out many times during this tough period. He loaned us money that we could not have gotten from any bank at the time, gave my family moral support and would always take the time to listen when I was having a tough time and needed to vent to someone. We are blessed to have him in our life.

I told Dean that God will never put more on you than He knows you can handle. Dean said, "He must think you can handle a lot."

So, I laid my burdens at the foot of the cross and walked away from the stress and worry. I have always prayed,

Lord, do not lighten the load, just give me a stronger back.

How God changes struggles into miracles:

Many people say that they don't see miracles anymore. I think that people are not looking hard enough for them. We have experienced more miracles than we can count. Many people say it is just coincidence, but we don't believe in coincidences. A perfect example of that is our friend Charlie Wolfinger. We know him from back in our high school days. Well, technically we were drag racing enemies back in those days, but we had both grown in our faith over the years and Charlie's walk with the Lord is one that I will always admire. We became close friends when I was going through my first heart problem. While I was battling my first heart condition, Charlie had a heart attack. His son, Chase, told me that while having the heart attack Charlie fell to his knees and thanked God for the heart attack. He said something good would come of it. And it did. Charlie and I would talk almost daily while we both went through our heart problems. And because of his heart attack we became closer than we had ever been. He strengthened my walk with the Lord. He would drop by or call and every time we talked and prayed together.

One afternoon we were trying to figure out how we were going to pay bills and my good friend Charlie Wolfinger walked into our store. We didn't know he was coming. We had been praying for guidance in the troubled time and Charlie Wolfinger walked in and said Steve I don't know why but I was on my way to get a new truck and I had the check in my hand to buy it and the Lord told me to come by and see if you could use it. Charlie had no idea we were struggling or praying for help, but the Lord knew that we needed his help. Charlie loaned it to us and said, "pay it back when you can." We tried to pay him back in payments a couple times, but he told us that if we can't pay it all back at once then we must still need it. So just wait until we get on our feet enough to pay it all back.

Another example is a year or so later when things were tight my aunt Donna came by to visit. We told her that things were still tight, but we were trying to hang on. She repeated what she had told me many times, "Steve if you need financial help, please call me and let me help you." So finally, one day I called and met with her and her husband, Dwain, and they eagerly helped us. Dwain told me to pay it back when I could, not worry about making monthly payments.

I tried to make payments to Charlie, and he said, "Steve if you can't pay the full amount back at one time then you still need the money so don't worry about it."

The Lord has blessed me with such good friends and family that I am crying as I am writing about this. God is always there if you just open your eyes and heart to see him at work in your life.

Another example of God turning disaster into a blessing:

Because of the contractor that was suing us, we installed cameras in our stores and factory. Months later the cameras caught an accident with the fork truck. At that time the lawsuit was still going on, so we had not lost our insurance yet. When the insurance adjuster walked in, he acted as if we were in the wrong and it all sounded bleak. But after reviewing the surveillance video from the cameras we had installed; the insurance did not dispute the claim.

And because of the accident we added extra security in the form of pin code locks to our office and factory entrances. Prior to that anyone could walk into our factory from our showroom. Adding the pin code locks protected a toddler one day from getting back to our factory production area. The machinery, while running, is very loud so we would not have known he had wandered into the production area. The Lord knew we needed to make some changes. And he used the bad to create a positive outcome.

A Dark Time in My Life:

I want you to understand that just because we are Christians doesn't mean that Satan can't work against us. He has full reign over this world. One day he tried his best to take ahold of me.

I was sitting in my office on a Thursday afternoon. I was thinking about how much we had lost and the struggles we were going through and worried we would never be able to recover from everything financially. Satan was working hard on my mind that day.

My father Charles had passed several years earlier and without my dad there to help toss ideas back and forth I felt lost and alone. He was always there for me to run problems by and help me make decisions and most of all to let me vent my troubles.

After sitting by myself in my office for about an hour, I seemed to drift away. All I really remember at first was darkness. I did not feel like I was in the room anymore and I did not hear Kim or Alice talking. I didn't hear the roar of the machinery from the factory. I felt very calm. It was like I was somewhere else. I remember thinking everyone would be better off if I were not here anymore.

Lonely and depressed, I drifted into this dark place. I don't know how long I was in this state of mind, but I remember hearing a voice in the distance. It was very faint and as it grew stronger, I realized it was my dear friend Bob Duff asking if I was in my office.

I felt like I was pulled out of the darkness in a split second. And I was back in my office sitting in my chair behind my desk again. But when I looked down, I had my .38 caliber snub nose pistol in my hand, and it was fully loaded with jacketed hollow points. I always kept the pistol holstered and in my desk drawer. I do not remember getting the pistol out of the desk drawer, nor do I remember removing it from the holster; it shook me to my core.

Satan was working on me hard that day. I just thank God that my Savior sent my friend Bob Duff down the hall at that exact moment to pull me out of the darkness.

Bob knocked on my door and just came into my office, he said "Are you alright, bubba? Is something wrong? You look very pale and confused."

I asked Bob to sit down, and told him what happened, still holding the pistol. He immediately took the pistol from my hand, picked up the holster, and carefully placed the pistol back into the holster. Then he stopped and prayed with me.

We have always kept a pistol at the factory in my desk for security. Later that day, I walked into Alice's office and handed her the holstered pistol and told her to put it in her desk or somewhere and not to tell me where it was.

Alice had a genuinely concerned look on her face but said nothing, she just took the holstered pistol. It was a few days before I told Alice and Kim what happened.

To show you how God was at work that day, Bob did not have the pin codes to access the hallway to our offices. But he was able to open the door and come down the hallway looking for me. The next day we tried the door several times in different ways to see if we could get the door to open without the pin code to no avail. After talking about it, Bob said he did not remember opening the hallway door or why he wanted to see me.

Again, God was protecting me that day for sure.

We know that while the earthly problems we have here are insignificant to God, we are important to Him. I had a pastor tell me once that problems don't already exist, we create them.

And yet God says in Matthew 11:28 (NIV), "Come to me, all who are weary and burdened, and I will give you rest." This is one of my favorite verses. I find peace and comfort in his words.

My Health Declined Rapidly:

While I had a bad heart, I was able to maintain a relatively normal lifestyle with my medications. I still had the occasional irregular heartbeats, but I was able to maintain a normal life with only 20% ejection fraction of my heart for about ten years. This leads us to 2019. The doctors would always bring up a pacemaker, but I told them I felt okay so I didn't want it unless I started to feel worse. But by September 2019, I wasn't feeling as good as I used to. I was tired a lot, and after fighting for ten years, I finally agreed to talk to the doctor about a pacemaker.

September 12, 2019. It was just a normal follow-up with my cardiologist. Only this time I was going to tell the doctor I was ready to discuss a pacemaker. I had been physically tired and run down. He wanted to schedule some tests before we went any further. I was very annoyed. They had pressured me for ten years to get a pacemaker, and now that I was willing to do it, they wanted to do more tests!? I was upset but agreed to schedule the tests.

We didn't make it that far. The following day, September 13, 2019, I was utterly exhausted. I was sitting at the desk in the showroom waiting for the girls to finish up so we could go home. But when Alice approached, she said something was wrong and told me the top of my head was purple and I was going to the emergency room. I fought her like I always do.

"You have two options" she said. "Either I call 9-1-1 and you go by ambulance, or I drive you there myself. But either way you are going. Now which one do you want?"

And of course, I fought her on it. I walked outside to wait next to the van for the girls so we could go home. I thought they would just follow suit, but they didn't come outside. So, I walked back into the building.

"Fine" I finally relented. "I will go."

"That's good" Alice replied, "because the ambulance is already here." she said as she opened the door to let the EMTs in. I hadn't even noticed the sirens as they approached our building.

I don't remember a lot about what happened after that. I just remember being tired. Later I learned that I went through over a dozen tests while the doctors were trying to figure out what was going on. I would breathe like a fish out of water then would pass out, exhausted.

The doctors were looking at everything: my kidneys, my liver, my lungs, everything except my heart. They ran a pulmonary nuclear test of some sort that required them to fly in nuclear material on a helicopter as they couldn't store it at the hospital. They did chest x-rays, EKG's, and several other tests over the next 4 days. I was in the hospital for three days before they ran an echocardiogram test on my heart. Even then, the test was inconclusive.

Kim and Alice would stay up at night taking 2-hour shifts watching over me. I would start breathing like a fish out of water and would pass out. It was 2 days before Alice noticed that I would stop breathing when I passed out. We had to demand that the doctors put an oxygen monitor on me. When they did the nurses were very worried. They saw my oxygen levels dropping when I would "fall to sleep," and realized I was passing out. My oxygen would drop into the 80s. At one point my oxygen dropped to 57 which is unheard of. I would wake up gasping for breath which would make me hyperventilate. So, Alice and Kim would take turns reminding me to breathe when I would wake up so that I didn't panic and hyperventilate.

The nurses kept trying to explain the severity of the situation to the doctors but when they did their rounds it was usually in the late afternoon. And for some reason I didn't black out as much at that particular time. But they kept checking my kidneys and my liver. None of it made sense to us. My kidneys weren't bothering me. I couldn't breathe! Since I was in and out of consciousness, I had no idea that it had been days. I thought it had only been in the hospital for a few hours.

September 17, 2019. After four days in the hospital in my hometown of Evansville Indiana, the doctor walked in and said that they couldn't figure out what was wrong. So, they were going to send me home. Kim and Alice immediately unleashed on the doctor. "The man is blacking out every two minutes and you think that is, okay?!"

The doctor still wouldn't listen to the nurses, but an hour later, a nurse practitioner walked in. She saw me unconscious and apologized to Kim and Alice and said she didn't want to wake me up.

"He isn't asleep!" Alice told her. "He is blacking out," as she pointed to the oxygen meter.

The nurse looked confused. She walked up to me and waited a few minutes until I woke up and this time the girls didn't remind me to breathe, and the nurse practitioner watched me hyperventilate and black out.

Then Alice turned to the nurse practitioner "And they want to discharge him! We keep telling the doctors that he is doing this, but he has never done it when they are here, so they aren't listening."

The nurse practitioner agreed that something was wrong and was going to go talk to the doctor.

Thirty minutes later the cardiologist that was on call the previous weekend had walked in. He followed up with my case and after talking to the nurse practitioner realized that they couldn't send me home.

"We don't know what is going on." He told us. "I want to send you up to Indianapolis to have some more tests ran. I studied up there for a while. They have this test called a right heart cath. It can look at the heart differently—they have more advanced treatments."

We were relieved. They were finally doing something. We thought we were going to drive but then the doctor said that I needed to be life flighted. If they couldn't get the helicopter, then they would go by ambulance, but they were doing everything they could to get the helicopter. I didn't think it was that bad. I wasn't too sure I liked the idea of going all the way to Indianapolis. We had a business to run. We couldn't be away from the factory. I was telling the girls that I didn't want to go. Thank God that my good friend Lee had come to visit me. He talked me into listening to the doctors.

The flight was quicker than I expected. A little over an hour and I was there. I was confused about what the doctors were saying, nothing made sense to me. They kept saying something about doing tests in the morning. I didn't want to stay another night in a hospital. And if I was so sick that I needed to be flown then why were they waiting to do tests? I called the girls on my cell and told them I wanted to go home. They were still half an hour away.

They finally calmed me down and I agreed to wait until they got there to talk with the doctors, but by the time they arrived I was thrilled because the nurse had brought me something to eat. Since the doctors at home were running test after test, I hadn't been able to eat much of anything in four days. I was eating a burger and sipping hot chocolate when Kim and Alice finally walked in.

We still didn't understand why there was such a rush to get me to Indianapolis as they didn't do anything until the next day.

September 18, 2019. The doctors attempted to do the right heart cath. They said it was a normal procedure, that they do hundreds of them every day. But they had to knock me out slightly to do it. I didn't have a problem with that. I hadn't slept a full night through in months. I was ready for a nice solid sleep.

When I woke up a few hours later they told me the test was unsuccessful. Apparently, I have an abnormality; they usually go in through the right Superior Vena Cava in, but mine wasn't there—it is a strange birth defect no one had noticed.

They said it took some work to get the Cath in place but as soon as they started gathering data I went into Ventricular tachycardia. They pulled back and the v-tach stopped but as soon as they re-entered my heart the v-tach started again.

"Ventricular tachycardia or v-tach is a condition in which the lower chambers of the heart (ventricles) beat very quickly. Ventricular tachycardia occurs due to a problem with the heart's electrical impulses. The heart is attempting to beat so quickly that blood does not flow through the heart. This can lead to a stroke."[1]

As I said earlier, my heart had an electrical problem. My plumbing was excellent, no blockages in my arteries at all. But I had a wire loose in my heart. It is called a lower left bundle branch blockage. I had survived for years with it.

---

[1] "Ventricular Tachycardia," Mayo Clinic, Accessed April 25, 2022, https://www.mayoclinic.org/diseases-conditions/ventricular-tachycardia/symptoms-causes/syc-20355138

They didn't say if they had to do anything to calm my heart, but they were all very concerned about me. They had their suspicions about what was going on but without the information from the right heart cath they would be going in blind. Knowing that I already had one major abnormality that no one had ever seen before at that hospital, they were concerned there may be more abnormalities. They needed more information and mapping of my heart before they could proceed.

When doing a right heart Cath, the doctor would normally go in through an artery in the neck to reach the right side of the heart. Since I was missing this artery, or it had developed somewhere else, they would have to go the long way to do the test—through my groin. This was not desirable as it was more complex; no one at the hospital had gone all the way from the groin for the test.

At this point, we still didn't know what was going on. We were expecting the doctors to do a heart cath and probably implant a pacemaker/defibrillator. That is all the doctors back home had mentioned for the last ten years. We knew they needed better photos of my heart. One of the cardiologists that was the most experienced said he thought he could do the right heart cath from the groin. So, they scheduled it for the next morning; they wanted my heart to rest after the day's trauma.

We would have to wait yet another day. I was getting irritated, I hate hospitals, and I just wanted to walk out and go home. But Kim and Alice kept insisting I stay. I argued with them quite a bit before I finally gave in and agreed.

To any man out there that doesn't want to listen to the women in his life, just listen to them. While I felt tired and annoyed, Kim and Alice could tell something was wrong. They could see it in me. And if I had walked out like I wanted to, I wouldn't have survived the trip home. By 2pm that evening the nurses were frantic, but we had no idea why. Then they explained that they couldn't get an IV or an A-line in. They needed to get one in so they could give me the medication I needed in the morning. They had numerous nurses try. They even used an ultrasound machine to see my veins and arteries, but no luck. They couldn't even draw blood. We could see the nurses getting more frantic by the minute.

Shortly after their final attempt, the pulmonary surgeon, Dr. P., walked in and looked at a few things in my chart. Then things went crazy. They told Kim and Alice that they would have to go out to the waiting area. The room filled with people. There were machines and people everywhere. I was done. I don't know what was going on, but I was done. I was tired and done fighting. I told them all to stop. I could feel myself slipping and I knew I was done. I kept yelling as loud as I could to "*Stop!*" The doctor finally listened to me. Everyone in the room paused what they were doing. "I want to talk to my family. I don't want anything else done to me. I want to talk to Kim and Alice."

"We don't have time," the Doctor said firmly.

"I don't care. I want to talk to them now. Don't do another thing until I see them."

At that point they brought Kim and Alice back into the room. Their attitude was different. Something had changed. I don't know what, but something was different.

"We don't have a minute." Dr P. told the girls. "We must do this procedure to save his life. Honestly, this procedure needs to be done in a surgery room, but he won't make it that long. We don't have a minute. We need to do it now."

"I don't want this." I told Kim and Alice as they approached my bed.

Kim said through tears "You need to listen to the doctors."

I replied, "I am done."

Alice insisted. "Steve, please. You need to let them help you."

"I'm done." I repeated. "I am tired of fighting. I just want to go home to be with my Lord and Savior." I said through labored breath.

Alice wiped a tear from her face. "Are you sure that's what you want? I promised you before that I would honor your wishes. And I will do it. I will stop them right now. If that is what you truly want."

"It is." I sighed; I was so relieved she was listening.

"I will stop them right now, but you must look me in the eye and tell me you are done. Look at me, are you done?" I looked away and Alice said, "Steven, I love you and if you say you are done, we will stop this right now, but you have to look me in the eye and tell me you are done."

I could hear the emotion in her voice. She was trying to be strong, but I could hear her and Kim crying. And I couldn't do it. I couldn't look her in the eye. I didn't want to give up, but I was just so *tired*. I had never been that tired in my life. Each breath took every ounce of strength I had. After a few seconds of silence, she knew I couldn't do it and took it as my answer.

"Okay, then I need you to let them do their jobs. They need to do this procedure to save you. Please don't fight them. Please don't give up." Alice begged as she and Kim stepped back so the team could return to work.

The room immediately filled with people again and the doctor and nurses began working franticly. They put me into a medically induced coma to keep my organs from shutting down.

MY TRIP TO HEAVEN

I was tired of fighting for every breath. They had me on life support with machines breathing for me while I was in a coma. They implanted a balloon into my heart to squeeze it and help maintain it. I felt like I was laying in limbo just existing and felt so alone; I was too weak to fight. My soul was weary, I remember the feeling as my soul lifted out of my body. I felt my chest heave as if my body was trying to prevent my soul from escaping.

I could feel the inner turmoil as my weakened body struggled to keep my soul in its place. When my body could no longer hold on, I felt my soul snap out of its earthly shell, and my body dropped back down lifelessly.

The freedom I felt when I left my body was like being confined to a small room then being set free. Suddenly, I was on the ceiling looking down at myself. Kim and Alice were by my body. Machines kept my lungs breathing and a pump worked my heart as the nurses moved around franticly. I looked to my left and saw a glimmer of light coming through the ceiling; it was like a beacon or voice calling me, yet it was emitting no audible sound.

I found myself floating, drawn toward this light. As I drew closer the light grew larger until I was totally immersed in it. The shimmering light was like millions of little particles all around me. Each particle flickered like millions of

microscopic lightning bugs. There were so many that the light never faltered. It grew brighter and larger with each passing moment. It was like nothing I had ever seen. It was so beautiful and inviting.

I felt a warmth that embraced my entire being and I felt love like I have never felt before. It was like I was being hugged by Agape love. This is a Greek word that means a Love that was more than a feeling. It was a state of being—a perfect love. I had never felt so loved and so wanted in my life. That is saying a lot as I was raised by two wonderful, doting, parents that put me before anything else. But this was completely different.

At that moment nothing else mattered. All I wanted to do was go deeper into the light. I was totally engulfed in the light and love. But somehow, I yearned for more. I needed more.

Suddenly, I was no longer floating but stood up right on my feet. I was not sure where I was, but I felt like I was home. It was a feeling of complete belonging, of being a part of something greater than myself. Not just emotionally but spiritually and physically. It was like that thing we are all searching for had found me, was now a part of me, and I felt complete.

Then my head started pounding. The sound, or noise, was so horrific, like millions of people all talking at the same time. It was so overwhelming that I could hardly stand it. I put my hands over my ears to try to stop the noise, but it did nothing. The sounds were being absorbed through my skull and into my brain. Or maybe they were coming from my brain, I couldn't tell which, but the pressure was so intense that I felt like my mind was going to explode. Then as quickly as it started, the pressure was gone. The noise that was so deafening just a moment before instead sounded like the wind whistling through the trees.

I realize now that it was the sound of billions of worshipers praising God. Billions of voices singing and praising at the same time. I guess my mind took a moment to tune into everything all at once. I was so astounded that I fell to my knees and shouted, "Glory be to God!"

After a few moments I returned to my feet and was elevated high above a crowd and a massive city. It was as if I was standing on a distant hilltop, but it was not a hill at all. I was standing on a substance that was solid in form yet liquid in feel. As I looked around my perch, it seemed to be changing colors constantly. A warm and tingly feeling ran through my entire body head to toe as if it was energizing me. This was the exact feeling I had when the Lord healed me of my first episode of myocarditis.

I was wearing a robe, not of cloth but of something that glowed. I noticed I was bare foot and seemed to absorb the energy coming from the light that was under my feet and seemed to be everywhere. I felt more energized and connected than I have ever felt with anything or anyone in my life.

I felt a breeze blowing on my face. But it was not like the wind we have here on earth. It was more like pure energy passing through my body. I could feel my bangs move across my forehead, which was unusual because I have been bald most of my adult life.

As the breeze blew on my face, I caught a whiff of something that reminded me of honeysuckle in the spring. It was like the sweet morning dew covered honeysuckle that filled your every sense. It enveloped me completely. It was so sweet that you could taste its fragrant aroma.

The City of Heaven:

I am going to describe what I experienced the best I can. I will try to use things from earth that might help explain what I saw but I must be clear, there is *nothing* on this earth that could explain or describe the beauty and majesty of what I experienced while in Heaven. So, for example, when I say something was *like* translucent, shiny moon stone or the smell of honeysuckle, I am trying to help you to understand the beauty of it all, but it does not come close to what I experienced.

Looking down from my elevated position I could see what seemed to be a walled city, and I heard a voice say, "Steven, take note of all you see and hear."

This was no normal city. The walls themselves went on for miles and miles both upward and outward. They were more massive than one could imagine. Infinitely larger than anything on earth. The height of the walls was greater than any human could ever build. I was suspended miles above the city so I could see all four of its breathtaking walls at the same time.

The Walls

The walls of the city were made of pure, bright white glowing stone. Their tops were capped with long smooth stone that glowed with a rainbow of colors like smooth moonstone or mother of pearl. But it wasn't solid or stationary like on earth. It was alive and in a constant state of movement. The iridescent stones didn't simply reflect light, they *projected* light.

The four walls of the massive city joined to form a square. Each corner had a large square pillar with what looked like pyramids atop the corners in all their megalithic glory. The pyramids were like caps on fence posts, and they were slightly larger than the post itself.

These pyramids made the Great Pyramids of Egypt look miniscule. The glowing white moonstone pyramids rose hundreds of feet above the top of the wall, and their sides were smooth and shiny as if they were made from one piece of stone and just polished.

In the center of each wall was a gate. The gates were enormous and awe inspiring. For those standing at the gate it was like staring up at a 100-story skyscraper, only the gates were much taller. They were made of the same moonstone-looking multicolored substance, continually changing colors.

There were no visible hinges as the gates did not open outward like normal. They pivoted at their center to allow access on both sides of the gates. There was some sort of a sign or writing above each gate.

From my elevated perch I could see that inside the gated walls there were pathways that seemed to go on for miles all along the wall. The pathways were made of the same radiant substance as the walls.

There were only two structures inside the city walls. One I believe was where the people resided. This structure was as large as a city. Unlike earthly cities, this city was all one massive building. There was a courtyard that encircled the entire area. The residential structure went on for miles and miles both up and out. It was larger than anything on earth. It would house billions of people.

The Residential Structure

The residential complex was square in appearance with what looked to be an obelisk that rose to great heights in each corner. The obelisks were even higher than the pyramids on the outer city wall. They seemed to go upward to touch the illuminated skyline. The top of each obelisk was covered with the same material as the gates and top of the walls.

There was no sun in the sky like we have here on earth. It was more of a glow, an energy, much like the light I had followed.

The walls of the residence structure were made with billions of uniformly cut, arched, floor-to-ceiling windows or doorways, they covered the entire outside of the structure. The doorways and windows were so massive that the residents looked like tiny ants standing at the doorways.

There were countless levels of the structure. Each one had a balcony that encircled the complex. The balcony was clear like they were walking on glass or a transparent substance. It appeared as if there were billions of apartments in the complex with glass balconies to travel from one room to another. There were people walking about the structure, floor after floor.

There were people in the courtyard as far as I could see. Thousands upon thousands of people, in all directions. There were people of every race, color, and creed. Everyone was together with no hate or anger. And as I watched they seemed to grow larger in number by the second, as if more were arriving at their final destination. There were no Catholics, no Baptists, no Pentecostals, only believers.

The Temple:

There were countless people in a courtyard on one side of the residential structure and the people were all facing what appeared to be a second structure that sat between the residential structure and the wall. I can only assume that the structure they faced was the temple. I heard a voice say, "Steven, take note of all you see and hear."

The people were starting to gather, and everyone faced the pillared temple. They were moving like they were worshiping, singing, and praising God. Although I could not see their faces from my distant overhead view, they all seemed to be moving to a purpose. Their bodies were moving back and forth, standing, and kneeling in unison. It was almost like watching a breeze dance across a field of wheat in the summertime. They were all worshiping as if they were one. I felt that I knew them all and they all knew me. It brought feelings of indescribable peace and belonging.

Unlike the residential structure, the temple was different. As I focused on the temple it became clearer to me. But it was not a temple like we think of in our earthly realm. When looking straight at the temple you could almost see the depth of the temple structure. At first, I thought it was part of the wall, but I realized it was not touching the outer wall of the city at all,

The front had 12 glowing white columns with 24 flutes per column and inside each flute was the moonstone material. That supported an arched roof and appeared to have the same moonstone as the top of the walls. The front of the temple had seven rounded doors that were closed, resembling the design of the gates in the city wall, made of the same moonstone with constantly changing colors. The two doors on the outside had writing up the sides and across the top in the moonstone the other doors had no writing just a trim around it. The temple was only in 3D when facing it directly. The temple sat between one of the walls and the residential structure.

I don't know how I know the dimensions and facts that I am about to tell you. I just know that I do. It was like the information was uploaded to my brain. And no, I have not read the book of Revelations. So, I don't know if it is the same or not. I just know that the temple was 777 acres, or almost one and a quarter mile wide. It was bright white in color and like the entire city that looked like moonstone, it had a bluish white almost electric glow about it. It had 2,222 steps that appeared to be made of a high polished white marble cobblestone that were as wide as the temple itself.

The steps were separated into two sections of 1,111 steps by a landing. The landing was made of flat glowing cobblestones that changed colors constantly and each measured 12 ft square. The cobble stones were laid out in squared sections of 12 stones wide and 12 stones deep. Each twelve-by-twelve section was separated by a trim of smooth tiles that were six foot by six foot square with a black "X" that ran from corner to corner with a black line on top and bottom of the "X's." The "X" design separated the section of stones from the other.

There was a total of 1,000 sections of stones on the landing that numbered 144,000.

As my eyes followed the 2,222 steps and up the 12 pillars to the roof of the temple, my eyes were drawn to the sky where I noticed giant glowing beings that were flying over the city. They were guarding or watching over everything below. There were thousands upon thousands of them. They were flying in a row formation; each row going the opposite direction of the row next to them. They were the Angels of God. Each had four wings, although they did not appear to have feathered wings like you see in

earthly representations. The Angels brok
pattern and began to fly in a circular pa
and temple. I watched in awe as 28 of
down. These large glowing beings lar
sides of each door of the temple while the u
circling. The angels were so large that they almost
touched the top of the arch inside the columns. As I
gazed upon them, the temple and other structures size
made more sense as the angels were so large that they
made the people look small in comparison. One angel
turned its back to the temple facing the worshippers,
while the other faced away from the city towards the
other angel putting 150-foot distance between the angels
as they faced each other. They appeared translucent
having human faces. As the temple doors began to open
the doors began to change colors faster almost like
power was building up in them. Slowly the angles bowed
down on one knee and covered themselves with their
wings to show respect. As they covered themselves their
wing tips came to a point in front of them and seemed to
almost touch the other angels' wing tips. As the doors
slowly opened a powerful almost blinding light emitted
from the open doors of the temple and spread outward
to illuminate the entire courtyard. The powerful light
illuminated through the walls and engulfed the entire
area inside and outside the walled city where the people
were worshiping. I had to look away. I was unable to look
directly at the light. I cannot explain it, but I heard what
seemed to be a voice resonating from the light. I know
the light was the light or power of God.

The crowd of people in the courtyard were worshiping
God. It was as if the people absorbed the sounds and the

ght as if to empower them. Looking down at my feet the surface I was standing on became brighter and the colors moved faster as if it was empowered by the light being omitted from the doors of the temple. I felt energy running through my feet and my entire body everything around was empowered by the light. Even the animals stopped to bask in its glory and seemed to worship it. Yes, there are animals in heaven. The plants and trees seemed to bow down to the light. Even the walls of the city seemed to somehow gain power from the light.

After a short time, the doors slowly closed. The 28 angels moved up to the front of the temple all standing next to one another and they all flew back up at the same time blending in to the circular pattern with the others and they began flying in the line pattern flying as they were before the doors opened.

I did not know how to describe the angels until I caught a glimpse of a representation on the history channel while working on this book.

The representation of what a group of astronauts saw from the international space station is exactly what the angels looked like that I saw. I cried when I saw their image on the TV. The artist's rendering is so close to the angels I saw! There is no way to capture the magnitude and beauty of these beings. They were much larger in size than humans. It was as if they were composed of light or pure energy.

Heaven was the most beautiful and peaceful place I have ever seen, nothing on this earth could compare or explain its beauty. It was magnificent.

Animals in Heaven's Forest:

When I tell people of my experience, one thing they often ask is if there are animals in Heaven. The answer is yes.

While I was still elevated above the city, I looked outside the awe-inspiring walls and saw miles and miles of fields of what I would describe as flowers. But they were much more beautiful than the flowers we have here on earth. People and animals alike were strolling together and enjoying the beauty of it all. at that moment I heard a voice say again, "Steven, take note of all you see and hear."

I noticed that when the light was coming out of the temple, people and animals alike would face that direction and kneel very quietly as if to show respect to God. I looked to the right of the field and saw what appeared to be a great lavish green forest. It was mammoth in size and went on as far as I could see and then some. It had to be the cleanest forest I had ever seen. It was groomed to perfection. There were no fallen trees or leaves or weeds. People were moving through it unobstructed. The trees were in rows that resembled a perfect orchard and seemed to go on for miles and miles.

The trees stood so straight as if to show pride for the Lord. They were well-groomed and very tall. I would estimate at least 300 feet tall and at the very least 10 feet in diameter. Every tree was the exact same size in width and height. The leaves on the trees were dark green in color yet they seemed to change different shades of green every few seconds. It was as if the color were light emitting from the leaves.

I saw hundreds of what appeared to be caretakers of the area. The caretakers were about 15 feet tall and very thin. They were so thin that they almost appeared stick-like.

The caretakers had absolutely no resemblance to the people. They did not wear robes like the people. But instead, their very skin appeared to be like clothing. They scurried about almost frantically cleaning and grooming both the area and all the animals.

I thought to myself *I wish I was closer*. In the blink of an eye, I was standing at the edge of the forest, and I could see the animals. They weren't just wild animals but pets as well. I saw a lot of the pets I had throughout my lifetime.

There was ole Bloop, a dog I had at 10 years old as well as Mattie, Mega, Muffin, Bopper, and many others I had as an adult. I looked around and I saw a dog come toward me at a peaceful pace. And as the dog came closer, I recognized her. It was my best friend Bob's dog, Fancy, whom I loved very much. She was a great friend. I also saw his dog Buster whom I only knew for a brief time, but I am sure it was him. As Fancy approached me, I could hear her say "Good to see you, Steve." Her mouth did not move but it was as if I could understand her thoughts.

I heard another voice say, "Down here."

I turned and there was a beautiful collie dog that had walked up to me unnoticed. It was my next-door neighbor Greg Moore's dog, Laddie that had passed several years ago. Laddie would come over to our yard all the time and we would wrestle and play. I heard him say "I always enjoyed playing and wrestling with you. Thanks for the friendship you gave me."

Along with the people there were all types of animals. I recognized bears, birds, dogs, cats, horses, lions, leopards, panthers, monkeys, and too many more to list them all. But if I had to guess I would say that every kind of animal here on earth as well as many animals which I had never seen before. They were all standing, walking, and lying next to each other calmly. Prey and predator alike, with no confrontation at all.

When I was a child, and though out my life I would see an animal of any kind that had passed, and I would pray. "Lord, I pray it did not suffer and let it run free forever in your fields and forests of Heaven forever. Amen." Well, I saw the fields and forests and they were outstanding.

The animals were all living and walking in harmony with the people, and it was as if they could communicate with each other.

I remember thinking of the verse, "*And the wolf will dwell with the lamb, and the leopard will lie down with the kid, and the calf and the young lion and the fatling*

61

together; and a little boy will lead them" (Isaiah 11:6, NASB).

I also witnessed monumental waterfalls. I thought to myself, *I would like to get a closer look at the water.* And in the blink of an eye, I was at the water's edge. I heard a voice say, "Steven, take note of all you see and hear." The main waterfall seemed to fall from out of the sky. It was so high up that you could not see where the water was  coming from. It seemed to flow from out of the sky itself before flowing down to a gorgeous mountain side. The mountain was covered in lush greenery and breathtaking foliage that was 30,333 feet tall perfect in form not a brown or dead leaf could be seen anywhere.

The water that fell from the sky was miles and miles above the mountain top and seven miles in width and when it hit the top of the mountain it roared downward and crashed into protruding parts of the mountain side as if showing great pride in the power that God had given the flowing water. It then split off into what seemed to be thousands of smaller waterfalls. And as the water landed at the bottom it sounded almost musical as if to sing to the Lord. It then became this beautiful floating mist and formed into a great body of water that rose to the edge of the forest.

There was every kind of fish you could imagine in the water, I turned and could not believe my eyes as I gazed upon alligators laying along the water's edge, yet there was no aggression from any living species in any way, even people. People were walking around the water's edge. Everything was in perfect harmony. The color of the water was breathtaking and changed constantly. The mist of the waterfalls was an awe-inspiring site to see. I was captivated with what appeared to be multi-colored rainbows trapped inside them.

I heard a voice and looked down to see a goose standing beside me. I knew instantly that it was Garvin, a Canada goose that we rescued and tried to nurse back to health a few years back. He suffered from metal poisoning when we found him.

After two weeks and many trips to see our veterinarian, Dr. Kilbane, and outstanding staff at Advent Veterinary Clinic, we lost Garvin, but not without an all-out effort to save him.[2]

Garvin looked at me and I heard him say, "Thank you for all you did for me and for continuing to help the ducks, geese and animals as the Lord asks you too."

Because of Garvin, Alice and I felt the Lord wanted us to help his feathered creatures. After much thought and prayer, we started the Garvin Foundation, a waterfowl rescue named after Garvin the Goose.[3]

---

[2] Adventvet.com
[3] Garvinfoundation.org
[4] https://academics.georgiasouthern.edu/wildlife/

Since its inception the Garvin Foundation has saved many birds. And a human life or two as well as helping others find their way in life.

One instance, we were on our way home from taking a goose named Goliath to Georgia Southern University's Bird Sanctuary. Goliath had been shot and had to have his wing amputated thus making him non-releasable. We drove him down to be a part of their educational bird exhibit. If you are ever near Savannah, Georgia, I highly recommend stopping to visit and learn more about the creatures we share this planet with.[4]

We were driving through Atlanta when Alice received a phone call about another injured goose back home. Some people had seen the goose at a lake, and it had a badly injured foot. We could not help them physically because we were 7 hours away from home, but Alice spoke with the young man who called, and she went through the steps on how to capture the goose without harming it.

About an hour later and after many phone conversations the goose was captured. Chris, the young man that captured him, named the goose Harvey.

We told Chris to take Harvey to Advent Veterinary and ask for Dr. Kilbane or Dr. Ramos. Advent called us and Harvey was so severely injured that he had to be euthanized.

Later Chris told us his story. "I have to tell you this" he said, "I was at the end of my rope. I was tired of living, no one ever showed me love or attention my entire life, but

---

then I met Harvey the goose. He needed my help, and he seemed truly grateful that I was trying to help him. I picked him up and felt a love I had never known. A love no human had ever shown. I didn't care if Harvey pecked at me or even when he peed on me. I didn't care. All I wanted to do was help him. I had contemplated taking my own life until Harvey the Canada goose came into my life. I realized there were others like Harvey out there that needed my help and so I want to become a volunteer and be a part of the Garvin Foundation and help."

Chris was instrumental in capturing our next rescue, and he named her Willow, she needed a wing amputated So after rehabbing her for about a month we drove her to Carolina Waterfowl Rescue in North Carolina; they are a fantastic nonprofit organization that works with all types of animals and waterfowl.[5]

Chris's story was a real eye opener as we felt the Lord told us to work with His birds. We had no idea how it would affect other people as well or how it could possibly save lives and bring people to the Lord. The Garvin foundation also educates adults and children on how to interact with waterfowl and sponsors walk-arounds a few times a year where volunteers show how to prevent problems by cleaning walks around the lake areas, and by picking up fishing line, plastic, etc., to keep waterfowl injuries down near our parks and waterways.

---

[5] https://www.cwrescue.org/

The Wall and Gates

My glimpse of the animals and the area around them came to an end as once more I was drawn to the city. Specifically, to the gate of the city. I thought to myself *I would like to see them up close and get a better look at the gates and walls.* Suddenly, I was in front of one of the oval gates standing outside the walled city. A voice said, "Steven, take note of all you see and hear." As I mentioned before, the massive oval gate would pivot at the center as if a dowel were in the middle of the gate. There were no hinges of any kind to be seen. The design allowed one gate to open and work as if there were two. One could enter or leave on either side. Each gate had markings above it and down both sides of the gate opening. When the gates were closed, they showed no visible signs of a gate, they seemed to become part of the wall again with no cracks the only way you could tell where it was located was the writing over the top and down the sides of where the gate should be.

I could finally see the walls of the city up close. They were made of a sort of pure, bright, white glowing stone. The stones were massive in size and were cut to fit together perfectly without the need for mortar.

These boulders or stones were of all shapes and sizes. The smallest stone that I could see was at least 100 feet in size. They were all polished smooth. The massive stones were interlocked and so precisely cut it appeared that not even a feather could fit between them.

The cut of the stones resembled the megalithic walls built by the Inca of ancient times only much larger in size. But the stone itself was unlike anything on earth. I leaned forward and reached out and touched the stone wall. The wall itself was smooth and felt warm to the touch. The stones felt solid but when touched it shimmered and rippled as though it was liquid. The entire wall was giving off a vibration that was almost musical. It was as if the walls of the city were giving praise to God along with the worshipers.

It was at that moment that I realized what I had been seeing. The people in the city and the people walking among all the animals and the birds and waterfowl and fish everything I had seen became clear: I understood that Jesus died for our sins, and I felt at that moment every animal on the planet as well. Salvation for *every soul* through the blood of Jesus Christ.

The feeling of gratitude I felt at that very moment was so overwhelming that I fell to my knees and cried out "Praised God the Father and Jesus the Son of God, for I understand that Jesus sacrificed himself to save all. Man, and animals alike." I cried and shouted as loud as I could, "Jesus is Lord of all!"

THE PEOPLE:

As I returned to my feet, the gate I was standing by started to open, as it opened there was a crowd gathering outside the walled city in front of the gate about 15 feet from where I stood. Everyone seemed to be in their mid-30's to early 40's, and everyone looked healthy, beautiful, and happy. Again, a voice said, "Steven, take note of all you see and hear."

I did not see any lines of people or souls waiting to get in. I believe, from what I saw and experienced, that you do not stand in a line. You are just there, no waiting, no checking in. You are just there, and you are known by all the very second you arrive.

The first to approach me was my father and my mother, Charles and Virginia Pike. They did not float or walk in. But one moment they were just there. My dad smiled and showed me his hands wiggling all his fingers. This was significant because he lost his index finger at the age of 6 when he fell 85 feet from a clay embankment, but he had his finger back.

I looked down between my dad and mom to see my dog Big Mac; he was sitting next to his brother we affectionately named Little Man. Big Mac was sitting there rocking back and forth on his front paws so happy to see me. He passed almost 30 years ago.

As I mentioned earlier, he was the closest thing to a son we ever had. It was like I could hear his thoughts as if to say, "It is so good to see you again."

I would like to pause here for a moment and touch on a subject that I have heard many people debate over the years. It was my parents' wish to be cremated so we followed their wishes. I have heard people over the years say that they believe that if you are cremated that God can't put you back together. Well, first, the bodies I saw were not like these earthly bodies. But for the sake of argument let's say you get your earthly bodies back. If you think God can't put you back together again no matter how you die, then you are putting limitations on a God with no limitations.

A pastor Bill Peroni in a sermon once said, "Before there was embalming you were simply wrapped in a cloth and buried in the ground. Now for the sake of discussion let's say an apple tree grows next to where a person is buried, the roots of the tree absorb your body for nourishment and then you become part of the tree, the tree bears fruit. The apples then fall from the tree. People pick them up and eat them, then they go off in different directions. They digest the apples and eventually the apples wind up in the sewer and spread into the water system. You are saying that God can put all of that back together, but He cannot put a person back together that has been cremated? God can do anything. Who are we, His creation, to put limits on our creator God?"

Back to our story. After my parents' arrival, one by one, more people came into view. I saw my grandparents, Joseph Earl and Alice Pike, Elmer and Kathryn Kasbohm, and many of my aunts and uncles.

I looked up and my Uncle Dwain was standing with a large group of people. He was smiling at me and seemed so happy. He was such a good man. I had only known him in his later years as he didn't meet my Aunt Donna until he was in his 60s. As I gazed upon his smiling face, he looked to be in his 30s or early 40s. I had never known him during those years of his life, but I knew it was Dwain. Once again, some things don't have to be explained in heaven, you just know. And I knew him. I knew Dwain the moment I laid eyes on him. I felt his presence before I even saw him. He passed away in November 2017.

As more people came into view, it seemed as if they were all appearing out of the massive oval gates to see me. The crowd seemed to keep growing. It was as if I was looking at my lineage back to the beginning.

I saw my uncle Jimmy in heaven. I mention him specifically because he had received a kidney transplant in the early 80s. He had to have a kidney transplant because he was an alcoholic and his kidneys had failed.

I remember as a small child of seven or eight my uncle Jimmy, my mother's brother, would call from California. Jimmy made a living picking fruit out there and would tell my mother that he wanted to come home and straighten out his life.

Time and time again I witnessed my mother and father send him the money they had put back for rent to help him come home. We would drive down to the Western Union station, and mother would wire him the money.

Jimmy would take the money and spend it on alcohol and a few months later call and do the same thing all over again. My mother continued to help him in hopes that one day he would come home and straighten his life out and he finally did just that.

At the time of Jimmy's passing, he was the longest living kidney recipient. He battled his addiction for years after his transplant. But sadly, he relapsed and started drinking again which caused his donor kidney to fail. He was told he was going back on kidney dialysis.

Jimmy told his family that the dialysis was the most painful thing imaginable, and he was not going to go through it again. Shortly thereafter he took his own life.

Many people of different beliefs may not agree with me, as they think if someone commits suicide they will go straight to hell. If you feel and believe that way, please do not let that stop you from reading on. There is an especially important message for every soul from our God in this book.

I know that I saw him. I know that God loves him and when my Uncle Jimmy accepted Jesus as his Savior, Jesus did not put a single limit on his salvation.

As I looked around everyone was smiling at me. They were all dressed in what appeared to be white robes. The robes had pleats running vertically from head to foot. While it appeared to be a robe it was not made of cloth but almost an electric bluish white haze around them and it covered their entire bodies. Only the neck, head, and hands were visible.

Next, I started to see friends, one after another. One of which was Rick Ramberger. He was my friend Bobby's father who lived down the street from where I grew up.

Rick worked for us for several years and I knew him well. Rick was an unbelievable singer. He taught me how to use the vibrato in my voice. He used to sit with his guitar and play and sing. He could have been a country star if he wanted. He sounded like a combination of Hank Williams and Randy Travis. He always had a kind word and never became upset with me even as a pesky kid who drove him crazy, always asking him to play and sing. I remember

71

when he passed thinking how Heaven had received such a fantastic voice for worship.

Rick was smiling at me and looked excited to see me. I could hear him speaking yet his mouth was not moving. "Hi guy" he said in his simple soft country manor. This was how he greeted me every time I saw him.

He said, "We do get to watch over those on earth occasionally." He continued, "Please tell my son Bobby to stop dwelling on what he did or did not say to me the last time we saw each other. Tell him to focus on Jesus and we will have eternity together to catch up." Later, when I returned home from the hospital, I met with Bobby to give him the message. He became very emotional and knew exactly what I was talking about.

I saw my best friend of over 50 years Odie Carrier who was murdered November 12, 2018. He looked at me and smiled. I remember thinking this place is so beautiful. That is when I heard Odie's voice say, "I know right," Odie used to say that a lot to me when we talked.

While at Odie's sister Theresa's funeral in 1996, Odie followed my wife Kim and I out into the hallway and asked us if we had a minute to talk, we said sure, Odie ask us what you had to do to be saved by the blood of Jesus. Kim, Odie, and I knelt right there in the hallway and Odie gave his life to Jesus, He cried and cried afterwards. It felt so good when I saw him in Heaven.

Odie looked at me and smiled and he asked me to tell his son Bobby and daughter Tiff to find a Bible-believing, grace - teaching church, and to get involved and take along the grand kids so they could all be together again one day worshiping Almighty God.

Just to the right of him was Jenny, Odie always said Jenny was his soul mate. She passed several years before him, she was smiling and looking at Odie while holding his hand. I felt so happy for them, also standing just behind Odie was his sister, Theresa, and his sister Pam, along with Odie's mother and father.

I saw George and Dianna Williams. They were good friends of ours. George passed shortly after his wife Dianna in 2015.

My childhood friend, Tony Austin, was there. He accepted Christ while in high school. Standing by him was his sister Tina Austin who was murdered when she was a young woman and standing just directly behind Tony and Tina was their mother Hope Austin.

I saw a woman that my dad worked with. He called her Reenie. She looked as she did when I was a boy. Amazingly enough she was my dear friend, Pastor Bob Duff's mother whom I mentioned earlier. She worked with my dad. She was holding the hand of a young girl who looked to be about 10 years old. When I told Bob about this later, he told me that he had a little sister that died before he was born. He had never told me about it before because it had happened so long ago.

I saw a man standing close behind them and felt I knew him; I asked Pastor Bob if his father-in-law who passed many years before was shorter than Bob and was stockily built with darkish hair parted on the side and kind of slicked back. He said yes and he showed me a picture of his father-in-law and I recognized him. It was the man I saw standing behind his mother.

I saw my wife's father Lee Withers. Lee had struggled a lot in life. He was a hustler. He gambled playing cards and hustled pool his whole life. He was a card dealer at a club called The Dells years ago and still had some poker chips from the club. I am not just talking about his youth. He made a good living with it and supported his family until his divorce.

Later in life he was asked to move from his nursing home because of gambling with other residents. My wife Kim had a rough relationship with him.

While Lee was in a nursing home, he said, "Many good, helping, caring, and loving people have gone home like my doctor, Dr. Boil. They have gone before me. Why doesn't God leave them here to help others. Instead, he leaves people like me." Kim reminded him that God loves us all equally, His son died for us *all!*

It was not until he was on his deathbed that he told Kim he would accept Jesus. I was there when Kim told him, "You can con me, dad. But you cannot con Jesus. He knows if you mean it."

When Lee died almost 20 years ago Kim did not know if he really accepted Jesus or not. She worried for years about her dad's soul. And as I stood before him, he smiled proudly and said, "Let Kim know that I am here in Heaven."

I also saw her brother Greg standing next to Lee. Greg was what you would call a tortured soul. He was always

74

worried that someone was looking at him or judging him. He always seemed sad. Greg fought alcohol and drug addiction most of his life and he was very insecure. He could not even eat at a restaurant as a child because he felt everyone was looking at him. I heard him say, "Tell Kim I know she was always there for me, and I love her."

Everyone was smiling and looked so happy. All this was said without anyone talking. It was like we could hear one another's thoughts. I have to say that I was overly excited to see Greg looking so good.

More and more people were gathering. My uncle Ray Ling was standing there. Ray had a very checkered past to say the least. He was in a lot of trouble throughout his lifetime and was an alcoholic as well. Despite his sins Ray was one of the nicest people you could meet, at least when he was around me. He fought a lot of addictions or demons in his life. It was great to see him looking good, smiling, and happy.

Standing close to my Uncle Ray, I saw a little girl who said, "tell my sisters Alice and Jessie and our mother that I am their sister Margret. Tell them that I'm okay."

When I asked Alice about it later, she told me that six months after her sister Jessica was born their mother had a miscarriage. I did not know anything about the miscarriage. Alice's mother apparently did not tell too many people. Alice didn't know herself until almost a decade later.

I also saw a man who asked me to tell Alice he was fine, and he would meet her one day. Later I described him as best I could to Alice. He was a short, dark-haired man. I had never met him. When I mentioned him to Alice, she showed me a picture. I recognized him immediately. I said, "That's the man!" She told me it was her father who was killed in a car crash five months before she was born.

Many people had gathered; there were so many outside the walls of heaven to greet me that I could not begin count them all. But it was if I knew each one of them and they knew me. We were connected in a way that I cannot explain. I could feel their energy. It felt like a homecoming, like I was looking at my lineage back to the beginning. I was like a puzzle piece connected to a living breathing family tree going back to the beginning of time.

I felt as though I met three different sections of people, 1)those that I knew and recognized like my parents and grandparents, 2)those whom I had never met or even known about like Alice's father and sister, Bob's sister and 3)those that could send a message or prove God's grace forgives all sins like my uncle Jimmy who committed suicide and Kim's father Lee that was a gambler and hustler his entire life. We were all linked. We were all connected on a spiritual level. I became one with the body of Christ. It was amazing.

I never wanted to leave this perfect place. One of the exciting things for me was getting to hug my dad and mom, and pet Big Mac our dog. I was also allowed to hug my best friend Odie. The hugs almost felt electric, sort of like static electricity. It filled me with joy, warmth, and love; I did not want to let go.

I was never allowed inside the city walls. I attributed it to the fact that I was not going to be allowed to stay so I

"You cannot see My face, for no one can see Me and live" (Exodus 33:20-21, BSB).

don't think I was fully changed and therefore God was protecting me for I could not have survived the power of God shining directly on me.

I felt at home, and I never wanted to leave. All I wanted to do was go into the city and stay forever!

I heard a voice say, "Steven, you must go back. I have work for you to do."

I did not want to go back. I wanted to stay; I was *home!*

TIME IN HELL.

My Arrival:

I felt as if I was falling backwards. I was light as air, as if I had no weight to my body at all. The light, and the warmth of the city became so distant that I could not see or feel it anymore. I found myself in total darkness. Everything became black. A black that is more than just a color. This was a black that was void of all life and existence and was bone chillingly cold. I felt totally alone. I could see nothing, so I closed my eyes. This did little to comfort me, but it was all I could do.

Shortly after I closed my eyes I no longer felt as if I was falling. In fact, I just stopped. I didn't hit anything, and I  didn't land. I just stopped as if I were at a crossroads. Again, I heard the familiar voice that said, "Steven, take note of all you see and hear."

I felt as if I was being pulled in a different direction. I opened my eyes and found myself laying on my back, floating in air about three feet off the floor with nothing to support me or hold me up. I was just suspended there, motionless. I looked down toward my feet and I was wearing my hospital clothing again, but I knew I was not in the hospital.

The place I was in had little to no light. The light was not constant or powerful like before. Instead, it was cold and flickered like a burning fireplace in a dark room, it was nothing like the light I experienced in heaven. I could not see a door or window anywhere in the room. In fact, there was no entrance of any kind. The walls seemed solid all around me. The room seemed to be oval, not completely round but longer than wide in symmetry but like an oval-shaped dome.

Lying there on my back, I felt as though some invisible force was holding me in place. I could not sit up or move my body. All I could move was my head and neck, which enabled me to look around. As my mind adapted to my new surroundings the room appeared to be some sort of cave. But it was not like any cave I have ever seen before.

The walls of the cave appeared to be hard, black, and cold. They looked as if someone had meticulously carved peaks and valleys in a convoluted pattern many millennia ago. The peaks and valleys had long since been worn almost smooth and now looked like polished onyx.

Looking around the room the wall that was at my feet had a strange writing on it unlike anything I had ever seen. Not only in the unrecognizable language it was being written but also in the way it was moving. At first, I thought my eyes were playing tricks on me as they were still adjusting to the change in light to the darkness of the dimly lit cave, I found myself hovering inside. The writing was being etched into the stone wall starting at the top of the fifteen-foot wall. The text appeared to be moving and changing continually. As each line of text was completed from right to left, it slid downwards to make room for another line of text. And as the lines moved downward, it filled the wall from top to bottom before the text slowly disappeared into the floor. It was like a line of eerie movie credits in a foreign language that rolled in reverse.

The unfamiliar letters were written out slowly and meticulously as by an unseen hand from right to left. The crimson blood-colored letters would spark like hot iron forged in a fire sizzling on the cold wall in an almost liquid form and hardened as it scrolled down to the floor. I could not understand how it was being etched into the stone wall,

I did not recognize it at the time but when I researched it later, I found it was similar in shape to ancient Hebrew but not exact. This is the closest reference I found.

At this point, I wasn't sure where I was, but I knew I was not in Heaven anymore. Unlike the first place I visited, this did not feel like home.

I was overcome with the feeling of fear and the need to flee the cold and eerie room but there were no windows or doors for an escape. I was immobilized, laying on a table that did not exist, being held down in a room with no way to enter or exit.

You would think that the room would have dirt like a cave, but it was immaculately clean. Not a spec of dirt was to be found. Even the embers of the writing left no ash as it continued to build the list at a steady pace.

Encounter with Satan:

I was still trying to process what I was seeing when it seemed out of nowhere a man walked up to me. I did not see how or even hear him enter the room. Suddenly, he was just there.

His appearance was outstanding. He didn't look like he belonged there. The man seemed out of place somehow. He was the most handsome, immaculately well-dressed person I had ever seen. I could not take my eyes off him. I still cannot quite put my finger on it but something about him drew me in. His dark black hair was flawlessly groomed and slicked back with no part, and not a hair out of place. He was clean shaven, and his bronzed complexion was perfectly complimented by his dark eyes.

I would guess him at about six foot six and about 225 pounds with a very thick neck and a muscular build. He wore a shiny black three-piece suit with a bright red pocket square or handkerchief perfectly folded into what is called a Dunaway fold. He wore a black shirt with gold buttons that  had some sort of a red emblem on each button. And was adorned with a gold and diamond collar bar that ran horizontally holding down the shirt collar points perfectly.

Running between the collar and the vest was a precisely centered and perfectly knotted solid red tie.

It was not just any knot but was a complex and beautiful Eldredge Knot. A knot so intricate that few people even know what it is let alone how to tie it. I had to research it myself to find out what it was called.

This elegant tie was held to the shirt with a gold and diamond tie pin about the size of a quarter. Between the collar bar and the tie pin were three small, thin, gold braided chains that hung from under the collar of the shirt out and over the tie. The bottom chain had a small gold medallion with red shiny writing on it in a language I could not read. His shirt sleeves extended out past the end of his jacket about 4 inches, and you could see the gold and diamond cufflinks that adorned his wrists. He wore a gold braided chain around his left wrist with small white pendants that appeared to be made of polished shiny bone. As he moved, a gold ring flickered on the index finger of his right freshly manicured hand. Everything, including the jewelry, was impeccably tailored to fit him. His black wingtip shoes were even edged with gold braid and polished to a high gloss.

He was the epitome of what we would call perfection. I remember thinking this perfect man was out of place in this dimly lit cave. Yet, there he stood. And with every ounce of sophistication that matched his appearance he said, "Welcome Steven. Would you care for a beverage?"

At that moment I was able to sit up. The force that held me down was gone. I was suddenly so thirsty that I didn't even think about how I had been immobilized until he came into the room. Realizing how thirsty I was. I replied, "Yes, I would like some cold water." It all felt surreal. "Who are you and what is this place? Where am I?"

He smiled and said "That's not important right now. What is important is getting you something to drink and to make you comfortable. All you need to do is simply follow me."

I asked him where we were going. To which he simply replied, "To my home."

Again, I asked him, "Who are you?"

He repeated "That's not important all you need to do is follow me."

Feeling the thirst growing stronger I stood up to go with him. As I stood up I felt a cold like I had never felt ever in my life. I was shivering clear down to my bones. Somehow, I knew that I should not go with him. That is when he looked at me and once more instructed, "Simply follow me."

I knew that something was wrong. I do not know how to explain it, but I knew I should not go with him. So, I refused.

He sensed my hesitation. Again, he repeated "Simply follow me." He paused for a moment and continued, "I will give you anything and everything you have ever wanted. I can take away all the painful things of your life and make everything just the way you want it to be or should have been. Your God let things happen to you that caused you great pain and suffering. I can take it all away, change your life, and make it the way you wanted it to be. All you need do is renounce your God and reject His Son."

He said this as if it were a small task. Again, with a deeper louder voice he said, "Accept and follow me."

There was the answer to my questions. I knew without a doubt I was talking to the Devil himself. I was talking to the fallen angel, Satan. He was trying to deceive me and trick me into renouncing my Jesus.

I felt totally confused by his appearance. He did not look like anything I had ever heard of. None of the Hollywood dramatizations of a person with red skin, horns and a pitchfork were there. There was no pointed tail or forked tongue. How could this handsome sophisticated man be the Evil One? The man before me was the opposite of all the things we have heard Satan was supposed to be.

Once again, he asked me to renounce my God and His Son as my Savior. And again, I refused. This time I said, "I am a child of God and Jesus is my savior."

He became terribly upset. He started shouting and screaming in a language I had never heard, nor understood. It scared me dreadfully. I tried not to show it. So again, I said, "I am a child of the God Most High, and Jesus the Son of God is my Savior."

He became even more upset. His image became distorted. This perfect man I had been looking at, the one who was immaculately dressed, well-groomed, and very sophisticated was transformed into the most hideous creature imaginable. It was as if in his anger he lost control over the projected image of beauty he wanted me to see. And for a second his true, grotesque face was visible. It was almost like his beauty was a hologram

84

breaking apart or a pixilated image distorted. As if the creature was trying to take over the perfect image I had been looking at.

The creature moved so quickly that it was just a blur of blue, red, and black. Then in the blink of an eye he was back to the projected image of perfection again; he was back to the same calm, collected, immaculate man as before.

Knowing that I was in the presence of such evil I knew the one thing that could conquer evil. I took a deep breath before saying with more force, "I am a child of God! and Jesus is my Lord and Savior! I will not renounce them. I will not rebuke my God!"

He lost control again and became the blurred creature. I realized that he never called Jesus by name. He always said, *"the Son."* Every time I said Jesus' name, he would lose control over his perfect image and for a fleeting moment I could see what he really was.

He returned to the beautiful image again. He was not upset or frustrated. In fact, I wondered if he even knew that I had glimpsed his monster within.

Pain and Torture:

With the wave of his hand, I was laying back suspended in the air being held in place by some unseen force as if I were on a table again.

He reached over and grabbed my hand. I was able to see the ring on his right index finger up close. It was engraved with an emblem that resembled an upside-down triangle with two entwined snakes under it. As he grabbed my hand he calmly said "Rebuke your God. Renounce him."

The pain from just his touch was so horrendous that I cannot begin to describe it. It felt as if every nerve in my body was on fire.

"Turn your back on His Son and accept me or I will inflict pain upon you such as you have never known."

Once again, I yelled, "I am a child of the God Most High, and His Son Jesus is the Lord and Savior!"

He reached out and grabbed my right hand and with one fluid motion, pulled all the skin and muscle off my hand. I looked at my hand and all that was left was bone. There was blood on the floor as well as blood dripping from the meat and skin he was holding that just seconds prior was my right hand. Oddly enough, I was not bleeding, it was like the wound had been cauterized the second he pulled the muscle and skin off my hand. He just wadded up the bloody skin and muscle and threw it to the floor. The pain was excruciating. My mind was reeling from what just happened.

Before I could say a word, he reached out and with one touch he took the bones that made up my hand. It was as if he simply pulled them apart and took them off my arm. He turned and walked away from me, stopped, turned back and smiled at me. Then, with a horrifying laugh he held up the bones of my hand and as he dropped them to the floor, the bones just fell apart on a molecular level until they were dust.

He again demanded, "Renounce your God and His Son! Accept me and I will stop the pain."

I refused again, saying, "My God is the one true God, the Father, the Creator of all things Heaven and earth. And His Son, Jesus, is my Savior. I will never renounce either one of them!"

I was in such pain and agony that I fought to remain conscious. I thought to myself, he may have taken my hand, but I knew he could never take my God from me. The pain and anguish were making it difficult for me to keep my focus.

He walked over to me, reached out and calmly touched my arm, and my hand was returned just as it was before. Immediately the pain was gone.

He scowled as he said, "you just witnessed my mighty power, I can cause you great pain or I can give you all the pleasures you desire. I can give you everything you have always wanted. I am more powerful than your God. I am the true god. All you need to do is renounce your so-called God and follow me."

Again, I refused and cried out "Jesus is my Savior!" He became enraged again and fought to keep his image together.

The room was getting warmer and warmer. As I lay there, I became so thirsty that I could not swallow anymore. My throat felt like it was full of powder or fine dust. I could hardly breathe.

It was like an enormous weight had been placed on my chest. He offered me water and to remove the pressure from my chest if I would reject my Lord and Savior. Not being able to speak, the only thing I could do was shake my head no. My throat was so dry, I could not speak.

"I can inflict pain upon you to which you cannot imagine nor escape," he threatened. He proceeded to show me the most horrible moments in my life, only it was a thousand times worse than it had been in reality. The images he thrust upon me were not on a screen. It was like he was playing them in my mind; they were so vivid that they seemed real. It seemed more real than reality. I could feel, smell, and touch the things I saw as if they were real. Every horrible decision I made was played over and over in agonizing torture. I relived the pain of each one. Then he magnified the emotional pain they inflicted by ten. Every dark moment was relived over again in vivid detail. I closed my eyes, but it did no good as the images were in my mind. The smells burned my nose and the sounds echoed in my ears. I wanted it to stop, but he kept going nonstop for what seemed like hours.

It was like he could reach into my soul and get every decision and twist it to be more wrong and more painful. Every decision big and small he could manipulate. He tried to make me feel like I would be held accountable for those decisions on my judgement day like I had never been forgiven. He made me feel as though I would be punished for things I was not proud of. He made it feel like when I was judged for those decisions that I would be condemned to hell. And the fear of that punishment was greater than any other.

Then he changed the images. "I can take you back and undo every one of those things. I can make it all the way you wanted it to be," he said as the pain from those images went away, and I was back in the same moments only this time the bad decisions were gone. The hurt and agony were gone, and all the regret was gone. Everything turned out like I had wanted it to in the past. He was trying to make me feel as if he could change the bad things in life so that my judgement would not land me in hell. As if choosing him over Jesus would ensure my eternal comfort.

In that moment I could understand why people would want to follow him. If he could really take away the painful things in life, then we could live a life devoid of regret. But I knew that it was only temporary. I knew that even if he *fixed* the regrets of the past that I would end up spending eternity in hell. I would have to give up God and Jesus to get that perfect earthly life. A few years lived on earth with no regrets only to spend eternity in the mental and physical hell Satan had created here wasn't worth it.

I thought to myself, *I will never renounce my God or His Son Jesus*. He went crazy and started screaming and hollering once again speaking in the language I did not understand. It was like he could read my mind. I tried to remain calm and not let him see or feel my fear.

Then suddenly without any warning, he let out a loud scream before disappearing. His voice was deep and garbled with an earie kind of howling echo. It was the evilest sound imaginable. It shook me to my core.

The room became so cold that it felt like blistering heat. He then disappeared into the darkness. I lay there wondering why I was there and what it was I was supposed to be doing. I could not understand what this was all about. Moments before this I was in heaven. I had felt the most perfect love imaginable. But now I was being interrogated by Lucifer himself.

All I knew for sure at that point was that I was not going to stay in this place. I did not belong in hell. I had been to Heaven and was told to go back, that I had work to do, but I was very confused.

I know I was not condemned to hell. I had accepted Jesus as my Savior and did not belong there. I was saved through Jesus' precious blood that was shed at the Cross of Calvary.

The Man in the Hospital Gown:

As I dropped my eyes from the black onyx ceiling, I noticed there was now an opening on my right-hand side that was not there before. I could see a hallway or pathway and I saw a man in a hospital gown. Satan had his arm around the man's shoulders as they walked together.

They were talking and laughing as they walked toward the darkness. My voice was weak and gritty from a dry mouth. Struggling to sit up I yelled out, "Satan get away from him!" I tried to tell the man to flee, that Satan was not who he appeared to be.

Satan slowly turned around from the man, leaving the man standing by himself, and Satan walked toward me. As he approached, I was still struggling to get up and I was pulled back down by an unseen force and again flat on my back. He reached over with his hand and touched my throat. It was as if he pulled out my voice box. I could not speak. I kept trying but I could not talk or make any sound at all.

No matter how hard I struggled I was unable to warn the man. I was forced to watch in silence as they walked off into the darkness. Satan turned his head and smiled back at me as if to laugh at my failed attempt.

I felt so disappointed. I felt like I had failed the man somehow and let the Lord down as well. To this day, I still feel deep sorrow and regret for not being able to help or warn him.

I do not know how much time had passed before he returned, but when he returned in his beautiful form, I could see Satan smirk as he touched my throat and restored my voice; he simply turned and walked away.

I felt like I was released from the force that held me down and I was able to sit up. As I looked around, I could see the opening from which Satan was entering and leaving the room.

Demons

Outside the dark room, I could see there were millions of small creatures everywhere. They were about three and

a half to four feet tall. They were all wearing long brown hooded robes that appeared to cover their entire body, feet, hands, and the length touched the floor. Around their waists were ropes with writing on them. The ropes were knotted in the center, and braided tassels hung about 6 inches from the knot. There was a round gold medallion with red writing on it that hung on each tassel. I was too far away to make out the writing.

I could not see their faces as they walked with their heads down. The robes were long enough to touch the floor, but they appeared to have no feet and glided across the floor as if they were floating. The bottom of the robe never moved or wrinkled as it normally would if someone was walking. There were millions of them everywhere working franticly.

I noticed that when Satan would move or step backward, they moved as if they feared him. They moved as if terrified of the very thought of touching him. Yet he controlled them without saying a word.

Then without any warning or reason the creatures began to come into the room. They floated silently and quickly across the floor and filled the entire room. I backed away from them, but they surrounded me and tried to grab at me. I was petrified, but something seemed to prevent them from touching me. They acted like they were more afraid of me than of Satan. I did not understand what was going on at the time, but I was grateful they could not get me.

I looked over at the doorway and Satan was standing there. He had walked away from the man in the hospital gown again and looked at me as if to get my attention. He then raised his arm and pointed to the man in the hospital gown. Without saying a word, the small creatures rushed out of the room and grabbed the man and drug him deeper into the cave. I was astounded at the speed of which they could move, the man was screaming for help as they dragged him off, his voice became faint like he was getting farther and farther away.

I felt so bad for the man. Again, I yelled "I am a child of the living God, and His Son Jesus is LORD and my Savior."

Again, Satan lost all composure and turned into the deformed creature screaming in the language that was foreign to me. Then he disappeared into the darkness. I was left alone again wondering why I was there.

My Conversation with Satan

Some time passed, and I felt the blistering cold again. I looked and once again he was standing next to me. I looked at him and asked, "Why me? Why am I so special? What do you want from me?"

"It's not just you that I want. I want every single soul. As many as I can possibly get." Then he smiled and started laughing. He continued. "You pitiful human souls build your churches and your temples. You build these buildings to worship your so-called God and you think that I cannot come into these buildings" and with a horrific forceful sound that shook the entire place he yelled in anger "Well your wrong! I *am god!*"

He laughed again loudly and said, "I am there walking in and out freely. Every service, I come and sit down next to those who are sleeping during the services. People who are not paying attention think they are safe because they are at church. I look for the ones who just go through the motions while at worship. They are so easy to transform because they are not paying attention.

He leaned in closer and almost whispered, "They are not listening". People think that they are saved by your so-called God because they show up on Sunday mornings and sit in the building. Those that think they are saved but have no clue that they already belong to me. They are easy prey.

He laughed again as he continued, "I especially like the ones who believe they are going to Heaven, but they deny Hell exists. People only want to hear about Heaven; they do not want to hear about my domain. The so-called pastors of your churches choose not to talk or explain my plane of existence for fear of losing members and money.

He stopped and looked calm and pleased with himself. He took a deep breath and sighed smugly. "Ahh money," he boasted blissfully. "That is another of my many tools. I can gratify human desires immediately with money. Whatever they might be, food, sleep, sex, drugs, pleasure, possessions. Whatever the emptiness is in your heart I use that to entice you. You humans are and have always been so gullible and easy to manipulate. All the way back to Eve.

Then he turned and looked at me, "I know what your desires and weaknesses are and use that to move people in the direction I want them to go." He became the most smug, arrogant self-centered person I ever came across.

He stepped closer as he continued, "It is so easy to tempt the flesh. Drugs are of my design. Once I have the drugs or alcohol in the flesh it will always be in the flesh. The person can stop using and think they are clean, but it takes very little to get them back again. I manipulate people with money to become drug dealers. Then there are the Taverns.

He took a step back again and looked pleased with himself as he sighed "Ahh Taverns. They are like Temples built to me. The ones who spend their time and hard-earned money in my Temple, I have convinced the flesh that by drinking and gathering in Taverns to party or have a good time as they say that it is harmless. They have no idea they are paying ohmage to me. But knowing whether it is my temple or not I still have you. And I feed off it!" He said hungrily.

He continued, "Then there are those who stand on the corners and beg for your hard-earned money. They are of my design. They are mine and mine alone. I place them there. I influence them on what to do and how to do it. I possess them totally. I put them there to drag you down and mock your kindness. They are there to take your hard-earned money for their own pleasures and vices that I provide." He said firmly as he clenched his fist as if he were snatching money from me.

My mind was reeling from what he was saying. He was so pleased with his accomplishments. He sincerely enjoys inflicting pain and harm on us, but more than that, he *feeds* off our misery.

He continued again, "Your so-called modern human society thinks I am a joke, that I do not exist. That I cannot possess a person because I am not real. I make it so easy for people to believe this. I have taken your God out of your schools and your homes. I have taken family and responsibility out of your lives and replaced them with broken homes, I have given you a false sense of security and thinking. There are those who worship me and pay homage to me thinking that they will receive favoritism. Look around, do you see anyone I favor more than another? You humans believe you are so intelligent and that you know everything. Sex is my biggest and best tool. With God out of your homes and lives, parents no longer teach their children right from wrong. The women have sex with men they do not love, and the men are always willing. This leads to broken homes and lives without them even knowing what's going on. Humans are so easy to manipulate once your so-called God is out of their lives."

I looked upwards and once again cried out "Jesus is my Savior and the Son of the living God!"

At that moment I could feel God's positive power enveloping me. I don't know how but I could feel the prayers of people that were praying for me. Their prayers were like whispers that protected me; they empowered me to keep fighting. Satan was infuriated. The prayers were like hot acid burning his ears. He screamed so loud

96

in anger that it was almost deafening, I felt the blistering cold, but when I looked, he was gone once again.

I don't know why but since I have returned to earth, I can look at a person standing on the corner holding signs like, "will work for food," or 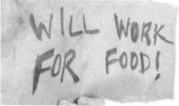 "please help," and I can see the demon in them. And they know it. The ones that are sent by the Evil One look at me and turn away quickly. It is a very eerie feeling to see them and know what is going on. Now please don't get me wrong not all of them are working for Satan. If you feel the Lord is telling you to help someone, then do it.

Levels of Hell:

As I stood there in silence, I was trying to figure out why I was in Hell. I was so focused on trying to figure it out that I had not noticed all the things going on around me. I looked around the room and noticed a new doorway or opening had formed out into a massive cavern. As I walked to look out, I again heard a voice say "Steven, take note of all you see and hear."

The inside of the cavern was the size of a city that went on for miles and miles in all directions. I could hear something like a thunderstorm. There were constant flashes of lightning and the roar of thunder. It echoed in the cavern and sent chills down my spine. This had been going on the entire time I was there, but my focus had been on my confusion of why I was in Hell and on Satan, not on my surroundings.

Then I noticed a stench in the air that was so horrible I could barely stand to breathe. It smelled like rotten meat and sulfur. I had to force myself not to gag from the putrid smell that seemed to come from everywhere.

I realized that I was finally able to move about. I walked to the round opening and saw millions of people walking out of a massive vortex and downward on this spiral path that went on for miles and miles. They walked side-by-side and shoulder to shoulder in lines of what looked like a thousand people wide. Each group was forced to stay in

place by one of the robe-wearing creatures. If they slowed or did not stay in the formation the robed creatures would lift their arm and a sword of bone would come out of the sleeve and it would pierce through the person, and they would scream out in agony. The blood spilled out of the condemned body as the person fell to the ground then the wound would instantly heal; this was performed anytime someone would not do as they were told.

The massive path was covered with broken shards of glass. The path spiraled downward like a staircase around a massive pit. The people on the path were barefoot and the jagged shards of glass were easily shredding their

exposed feet. They cried and moaned as they walked past the room I was in, and I noticed their skin started to decay the second they entered hell. They were forced to walk deeper and deeper into the pit. It took a moment for me to realize the dark crimson red color of the path was the blood from the cuts of the condemned souls' feet soaking into the dirt.

As they came out of the vortex into Hell they were met by the robed creatures and escorted down the path and into different levels of Hell.

I realized that the flashes of lightning were not lightning at all. With every flash it brought the arrival of new souls through the vortex in the wall. It was the souls of those that had given in to him or just did not accept Jesus as their Savior.

And the thunder I was hearing was the screaming agony of the lost souls crying repeatedly and gnashing their teeth. They were crying out for God to save them as they descended deeper into Hell.

That's when I put it together, the crimson blood-colored letters that sparked like hot iron forged in a fire sizzling on the cold wall behind me, the unfamiliar letters that were being written out slowly by an unknown hand from right to left, rolling from top to bottom and disappearing into the floor, was in fact a ledger of names of the souls of those being admitted and condemned into Hell. If there is a Lamb's Book of Life in Heaven, there must be the Beast's Book of Death.

I shuttered at the thought of all the souls lost. I remember thinking, *are we not doing our job as Christians? Are we failing that badly? Why are we losing so many to Satan?*

The small, robed creatures were ushering the condemned souls further and further down from the vortex deeper into the pit. This was not like any pit or cave seen before. It was massive. The pit itself was the size of a large city. There were rows after rows of people descending farther down the agonizing blood-stained path towards their eternal destination.

I did not see everything, but there appeared to be nine or ten levels, each level having its own opening or doorway. The robed creatures would stop at the doorway to each level and direct thousands of the people into the massive doorways at that level.

The room I was in was unlike the others. The room was big but not as large as the rooms the people were being forced into. There seemed to be no limit to the size of the rooms or the number of people they could hold. Those rooms were so large, they almost appeared to go on forever. But my room was more like Satan's personal torture room or office. Something that he reserved for his one-on-one interactions. Whereas the other doorways were massive and could accommodate thousands of people walking side-by-side.

As I looked down the hallway, I could see a massive entrance that was miles wide. It was about a hundred feet or so from where I was standing. The doorway opened to an even larger room. I was able to glance inside the massive room and the walls appeared carved out and convoluted like the walls of the room I was being held in. I realized that this was the first level of Hell.

The next level seemed blisteringly cold, but as the levels went deeper, each level seemed to get hotter and hotter until the black walls glowed red. Further down the walls became white hot. I looked in awe at the horrific sight as the thunder and lightning continued to usher in souls by the thousands.

As the robed creatures ushered the people into the first room, anyone who hesitated was stabbed with the bone sword that came out of the demons' arms. Once the group entered the first doorway, their clothes came off as the demonic creatures would force them down into a pit. There were so many people in the pit that they were squeezed shoulder-to-shoulder, they were overtaken by a wave of what I could only describe as molten red-hot lava. It would pass over them and their skin sizzled as it dissolved off their bones in waves.

The second wave would replace their skin, only to have the next wave remove it again. This happened over and over like an ocean tide flowing in and out. The agonizing screams were painful to hear. It was their never-ending torture. The smell of rotten meat and burnt flesh grew stronger with each wave. The smoke from their charred flesh filled the massive room before bellowing out and filling the cavern.

I leaned out as far as I could to see but would not step outside my room. I felt that if I stepped out onto the path, I would be marched down with the others.

I could see the entry way to the second level. As I peered into the opening, I could see people being forced off the spiral path and into the sunken pit—thousands upon thousands of them. I could tell it was extremely hot and everyone was crying out for water. The wall on the right side of the pit was clear like glass, and behind it water ran like a waterfall. People were crying and screaming trying to get to the water. They grew more frantic as they climbed over one another and beat on the clear wall in hopes of breaking it to no avail; they hoped for just a single drop of water.

As I watched this horrific scene, I realized that Satan did not have me. If he did, I would be marching down the pathway with the other souls. And again, I wondered why I was there.

I continued to watch as people filed past me in pain and agony. I was still wondering why I was there when I saw a dark-haired Caucasian woman lean on another woman of Asian descent try to help each other stay on their feet. As they walked past my doorway, the Caucasian woman turned to me in desperation while being marched down the path and she yelled at me, "Why does God not hear our cries for help?"

Looking at the floor to avoid the sight of the two women's decaying skin, I told her the heart wrenching truth, "He hears you but there is nothing left for Him to do. Until we draw our last breath, we have the freedom of choice. We can accept His Son Jesus as our Lord and Savior and live in eternity with Him worshiping the Father or not accept Him and live in eternal damnation. You made your choice. He can't help you now."

The woman responded, "I did not make a choice. I did not understand. I thought it was all just a story."

I replied, "By not making a choice, you made your choice. Not choosing Jesus as your Savior left you with hell, Satan, and damnation for all eternity." The woman begged me to help her. I felt so bad for her. If only she would have listened and accepted Jesus as her savior when she had the chance.

Then suddenly the small creatures that were ushering the lost souls down the pathway, grabbed the two women, and ran the bone sword through the woman I was speaking with dropping her to the ground the Asian lady helped her back to her feet and the creatures dragged them off into the darkness. I could hear her screaming as they escorted her deeper down into hell.

This terrified me. I yelled out "Jesus is the Son of the living God. He is my Savior, my Redeemer; I am a child of God."

Satan showed up again and with the wave of his hand, I was forced back onto the unseen table. Satan again took my voice away and left me floating on the surface as he disappeared into the darkness. I was flat on my back unable to sit up again.

I remember closing my eyes thinking, *you can take my voice, you can silence me, but you cannot take my salvation. I will never renounce my God or His Son. I have made my choice and there is nothing you can say or do to change that.*

When I reopened my eyes, Satan was again standing over me. He smiled and said, "If your God is so great why did He lie to you and send you to Hell?" He touched my throat again and my voice returned. Still pinned to the unseen table, I remained silent. He turned and walked away.

With Satan's back to me as he left the room, I could hear him say, "I can grant you everything you have ever wanted, more than anything I can give you the desires of your heart. Your life will become anything you want it to be, all you must do is accept me and this will all stop."

He let out a horrible laugh that seemed to shake the entire structure.

I asked, "Why would I want that, I have seen Heaven and it is the most beautiful place, a place of belonging. Why would I want to give up eternity in Heaven for a short life of luxury on earth and an eternity in Hell?"

He began speaking in the unfamiliar language again and I could tell he was terribly upset but said nothing more and just left the room.

I remember laying there thinking, *"Why am I here? Where are you God? Why did you let me get taken here?"*

I cried out in anger, "Why am I here! Why am I alone?!" Honestly, I was scared to death, but I did not want to let Satan see my fear.

I felt confused because all the lost souls were coming through the fiery vortex, but I didn't come in that way, I was in a room to itself and was just *there*, no fire, no smoke, no vortex or opening, just *there*.

The Answers to my questions:

I tried to sit up again this time with success, and I heard an incredibly quiet, calm, but forcefully deep voice that came from behind me "Steven, you're not alone! You have never been alone. I've been with you the entire time. I have been right here holding you, protecting you, and watching over you. Why do you think the demons could not touch you and were afraid? Why do you think he has become enraged every time you have said My name? He could see me here with you. I am here protecting you from Satan and this place."

I felt a calm come over me, so I no longer feared Satan or Hell, I felt the love and connection I felt in Heaven.

I don't know why but I felt I should not turn around. Still looking forward I asked, "If you have been here the entire time, why did you let him torture me?"

He responded, "Because you still have free will, you still have a choice. You could have renounced the Father and the Son, rejected your salvation and accepted Satan's offer, but you did not. You held fast to your faith and stayed strong. I could not let you know I was here with you as to not influence your thoughts or decisions."

I knew then the voice I was hearing was Jesus. He went on to say, "You will not be left here. I want you to tell the story of what you have witnessed both in Heaven and in Hell, so that others will hear and understand that there is a Hell as well as a Heaven, as the end time nears. The only way to Heaven and the Father is through His Son, Jesus, while under grace."

Then he added, "Go back as the Father has commanded and tell your story to anyone who will listen. Let them know what you have witnessed in Heaven and Hell, let them know they have a choice.

There will be those whom Satan will use to mock you. They will try to discredit you and your story, but do not let that stop you. This is the reason you were able to see Heaven, speak to people there that you knew and people you did not know, and given messages to take back to prove you were in fact in Heaven.

Stand strong and tell what you have seen both in Heaven and in Hell. Stand strong in your faith as you did here, for you are a child of the God Most High. Now go back to earth and do what you have been told to do."

The Shadow:

While I heard the voice, I never saw the face of the one speaking to me. He was always behind me. But as he spoke and told me to go back and tell my story, I looked at the dark walls of the cavern and saw a shadow rise.

On earth our shadows cast darkness as they block the light, this was just the opposite. His shadow reflected light on the dark walls of the cavern, no dark shadows. Which reminded me of being in Heaven and not seeing any shadows and thinking there is no darkness in Heaven.

As he talked to me, I saw the lighted glowing shadow of his hands reach out so I could see the holes in his hands—my Savior's hands. And the voice said go back tell what you have seen and watch your life unfold before your eyes. I am with you always.

My Departure:

Once again, I felt light as air. I began to float upward as if coming out of the cave. I could see the small creatures looking at me, reaching for me. They had no faces, just a skeleton, but somehow, I could see the disappointment on their faces as I floated past them. They were reaching as if to grab me but seemed more like they were trying to scare me as if they were afraid to touch me.

My Return to Earth:

It became darker until it was pitch black again like before I entered Hell, I could not see or hear anything. It was as if I were in a void that exists between heaven, hell, and earth.

After a few seconds, I could hear a faint beeping and people talking. The sounds grew stronger and clearer by the second. A bright light showed up that was so strong I had to turn my eyes away from it. I felt as though I was shoved back into my body by a massive force. I opened my eyes, but everything was very blurry at first. I kept blinking, trying to focus and after a few seconds, everything became clear. I was in the hospital bed hooked to all kinds of machines and monitors. Again, it took a while to understand where I was.

Coming Out of the Coma:

There was a loud machine at the foot of my bed that I was told was pumping my heart and squeezing fluid off my body. I was so tired.

They were trying to tell me what was happening. I was trying to tell them where I had been and what happened to me as the Lord told me to tell my experience to the world.

I was getting too excited, and I could not get them to understand me as I was still intubated and could not speak. I was even trying to use sign language when the nurse finally told Kim and Alice if they could not get me to calm down, they would have to leave, and the nurse would have to sedate me. So, I calmed down until I was able to tell them what happened to me. Every time I tried to explain my story, I became so emotional I could hardly speak. It was days before I was able to explain it.

While in the coma for two days, they pulled 30 pounds of fluid off me in the first four hours. My body weight went from 210 pounds down to 145 pounds in two days.

After two weeks of trying to stabilize me enough for surgery I had open heart surgery and had an LVAD (Left Ventricle Assistance Device) placed in my chest to strengthen my heart. I had absolutely no fear of the surgery at all, I knew the Lord was with me and would bring me through it flawlessly and He did. Alice and Kim kept everyone advised of my situation and had thousands of people praying for me every day throughout the entire month-long stay in the hospital. The prayers did not go unanswered. Later I realized that the prayers I heard in hell, the prayers that seemed to give me strength at my weakest moments, were the prayers of thousands of people fighting with and for me on earth. There is power in prayer!

My Recovery:

When I came out of surgery, and they got me back to my room in intensive care, I was trying to move my hands and feet and telling everyone to get me into physical therapy so I could fully recover; I knew I had work to do for the Lord. Every day in the hospital they had prayer over the intercom system which was amazing and encouraging.

Two weeks after my heart surgery, I was moved from Intensive care to a different floor called Cardiovascular/Peripheral Vascular Unit. This was the unit that transitioned transplant and LVAD patients from hospitalization to home.

Every morning there was a man who walked by my room, I assumed he was a heart patient and they had him slated for exercise as they did with me later. He passed by my door just out of my sight. I couldn't physically see him as I was limited on my mobility, but daily he said, "Hang in there, Jesus is with you, and you will get through this." I felt like the Lord had sent him to encourage me

109

and help me fight to get stronger. He went home before I was able to meet him and thank him.

They had me up and walking in just a few days and it was tiring. I could hardly stand, but I felt a presence there with me that lifted me up and pushed me forward. I remember while walking it felt as though I was being carried. I don't know how to explain it. I saw my feet moving and my body walking, but it was as if it was not me doing the work.

 I have always been strong willed, my favorite motto has always been, "Those who say it is impossible should stay out of the way of those of us who are doing it." I have always pushed forward no matter the obstacle, but this was a challenge and an all-out effort that I had never met before. God wanted this story to be told so I was going to get it done and had to get in shape to do it.

The whole month I was in the hospital, Kim and Alice had to make a tough decision to shut down our business. No one knew the day-to-day operations and I was shocked. They kept this from me so I wouldn't get upset. They knew I would worry about being closed for that length of time. Wholesale had slowed and finances were getting tighter and tighter.

Before I went into the hospital, unbeknownst to me, we didn't have the money for the girls to stay at a motel more than a night or two. They were about to start sleeping in the van in the hospital parking lot when someone mentioned The St. Vincent House for people that need a place to stay while their loved ones are in the hospital. Kim and Alice contacted The St. Vincent House and were able to get assistance and were given a room. The two would take turns going there to clean up and get what rest they could as one of them was always by my side the entire time. I just don't have the words to thank them for all they did and all they sacrificed to help me through my illness.

Another Show of God and How He Works:

Kim and Alice were offered the room at The St. Vincent House. While they were getting everything set, they met Tammy from Atlanta. Tammy was talking about her sister whose health had deteriorated rapidly. The sister had been admitted to the hospital and had no one to be with her so Tammy needed to be by her side. She explained how she had nothing, no money, no food, no place to stay, not even a change of clothing, and that she had quit her job to be with her sister. She had given up everything to be there for her sister whom she loved very much.

Alice and Kim prayed together and felt like the Lord was telling them to help Tammy, but they didn't understand how they could help her. Alice remembered that they had been carrying a $100 Target gift card in her purse.

At first, Kim and Alice were excited because they knew we could get things we needed. They were tempted to keep the card, because at that time they only had less than $5 in our bank accounts. However, they felt the Lord had sent them the gift card for Tammy and not for us.

The gift card was for redeemed credit card points a few weeks before we were in the hospital. Alice forgot it was in her purse. After discussing it, Kim, and Alice both felt that the money was intended for Tammy. They didn't want to take credit for helping Tammy, so they gave the card to the receptionist at The St. Vincent House and asked her to give it to the Tammy anonymously.

The receptionist gave the gift card to Tammy. When Alice and Kim ran into her the next day, she was excited not knowing they had provided the gift card. Tammy began telling them about how she was given the card and all the things she was able to purchase with the card.

 She teared up as she proclaimed how God had blessed her. Tammy was so moved by the kindness and miracles our Lord provided for her during this tough time. She put her faith in Jesus, and He provided for her needs. The girls never told her that the Lord had used them to bestow the gift on her. They just smiled and praised God for His mercy.

The $100 gift card made it possible for Tammy to purchase a clean pair of clothes, toothpaste, and a blanket to keep warm in the cold ICU room. They could have easily said we need to keep this for ourselves because they had no money at the time either, but they knew the Lord wanted them to help Tammy, so they did.

Shortly thereafter they received my first social security check, and the amount was $10 more than my insurance premium that was due while I was in the hospital so that left them with 10.00 to eat on.

They also had a direct deposit from one of the wholesale accounts that we had before we closed the factory, and that was enough to pay the utility bills to keep the lights on at home and work. This also gave them enough to purchase more food.

My problems were so serious that it took both Kim and Alice to stay with me in the hospital to get me through. As I said before, one of them was always by my side. Occasionally, one of them could return to the room at St Vencent House, but most of the time, they slept in my room in extremely uncomfortable chairs and monitored everything every step of the way.

I will never be able to find the words to show my gratitude to both Kim and Alice. I am truly a blessed man to have two such caring and wonderful ladies in my life.

After three weeks the nurse finally came in and told me I was going home. I was so excited. I wanted to get out of the hospital so I could get home and start on this book.

While we were waiting to be released from the hospital, Kim, Alice and I were praying and thanking the Lord for getting me through this and when we said amen, I heard a male voice say, "Amen." We looked up and one of the doctors was standing there.

I told him I wanted to thank him and all the people at the hospital. I said they were topnotch, and he replied, "We just do the work," he pointed up at the ceiling with his finger and said, "God does the healing."

After 5 weeks in the hospital, the doctors finally released me, and I was able to go home. I was so weak that I wasn't sure if I could make it up the stairs once we returned home. I called my dear friend, Pastor Bob, and he met us at the house when we arrived home that first evening.

I had a rollator—or a rolling walker—which had a seat on it, so Bob and Alice pushed me up the side ramp in the yard while I sat and held on. I was so grateful for all his help. Pastor Bob said, "I would have carried you up to the house if need be." He really would have; I have no doubt.

After getting inside the house, Pastor Bob helped me into a chair. I was trying to explain to him about my experience, and he could tell how emotional I was becoming so he stopped me and said, "You need to calm down and rest. I will come back, and you can tell me all about it."

While in the hospital and in the coma, my body had absorbed most of my muscle mass to keep it alive. I was so weak I had to sit at the sink and brush my teeth and that was an exceedingly difficult task. I could not even cup my hands together to hold the water to rinse my mouth. It took months of challenging work to get my strength back.

When Thanksgiving rolled around, I tried to help Kim and Alice in the kitchen. I always helped cook the meals, but I was so weak I could not stand. So, I sat down at the kitchen table and asked them to give me the cans of green beans and I would open them. Using a manual can opener it took every ounce of strength I had and seemed to take forever to get the cans open. I was so proud that I finished the task and it felt so good.

My recovery has been long and tiring but I pushed on every day. With the help from my rollator, I would walk just a little bit farther, push just a little bit harder, I would go to work, and I would walk around the factory and when I passed the stairway, I would step up one step and back down. After doing this for a day or two, I increased it to two stairs and did this until I could make it to the top of the staircase.

I just want to say something here. If you have gone through a heart surgery, illness or injury and are trying to recover, I have found there are two types of people: those that sit and worry and think to themselves *I can't do this or that anymore* and the ones that are going to live as normal a life as they can. You must keep trying to accomplish tasks small or large, it all gives you hope to keep pushing to get better.

Keep a record of your day-to-day achievements in a notebook or on video. Even little things like opening a can of green beans. When you feel you are not doing any better, look back at the accomplishments in the notebook or video, it will surprise you and motivate you. It will remind you of the things you have done and help you to push on.

Pray and talk with the Lord and ask Him to give you the strength and endurance even to open that can of beans or walk just a little farther or walk up that extra step that you could not take the day before.

I have been truly blessed and my recovery has gone well. I must wear batteries and a controller to keep the LVAD pump working, but I feel great. I have decided after much prayer not to be on the heart transplant list. I feel so good with the LVAD I don't want to take a heart from someone who is really suffering and must have the transplant.

The LVAD technology is just unbelievable and truly a gift from God along with meeting some incredible people along the way. Since my LVAD surgery I have become friends with an incredible person. His Name is Randy Thorton. He is a brother to me and has also gone through LVAD surgery. He has accomplished a lot in his life, he played in the NFL, was a pro wrestler named The Big Swoll, worked in the music industry with some great people and so much more, watch for his book on his life story it will be amazing. Having an LVAD has not slowed him down at all. No matter what hits you in life you must keep pushing forward Randy is a perfect example of live your life to the fullest.

As you have read my story, you may or may not believe what I went through, but I want to say this:

Heaven exists as does Hell. You need to accept Jesus into your heart if you have not already done so. Do not wait or hesitate, don't think that because you have not been perfect and have done bad things in your life that God does not want you.

That is what Satan wants you to believe, but God forgives, and His desire is for you to be with Him in Heaven. There were two criminals crucified for their crimes next to Jesus. One scoffed at Jesus and the other believed and Jesus said to him, "Today you will be with me in paradise" (Luke 23:43).

That's right! A criminal! Look it up for yourself. I have the verse written below, so no matter what you have done in your life, Jesus loves you and wants you with Him in Heaven. While I was there, I personally witnessed family members and friends there who were criminals, some were gay and some drug addicts, dealers, and alcoholics. God loves all of us and we have a new beginning once we have accepted Jesus into our lives. After you accept Jesus as your Lord and savior this does not mean you will never fail again. But under grace all is forgiven Jesus will not reject you. The truth is, none of us are worthy, *but He loves us all anyway.*

Luke 23:39-43

> One of the criminals hanging beside him scoffed,
> "So you're the Messiah, are you? Prove it by
> saving yourself—and us, too, while you're at it!"
> But the other criminal protested, "Don't you fear
> God even when you have been sentenced to die?
> We deserve to die for our crimes, but this man
> hasn't done anything wrong." Then he said,
> "Jesus, remember me when you come into your
> Kingdom." And Jesus replied, "I assure you, today
> you will be with me in paradise."

Everyone that I spoke with in Heaven had their own flaws and problems and sins on this earth, but they were washed clean by the blood of Jesus and yours can be as

117

well, all you need to do is accept Jesus as your Savior. Accept Jesus right now and your sins will be forgiven instantly. You can walk away from your old self and have a new beginning, do not wait any longer. Accept Jesus as your Lord and Savior, if you do not, and you draw your last breath before you accept Jesus, then Hell is your destination after death.

If you have been saved, tell anyone who is not saved. Talk with them and help them find their way to Jesus. Show your hope and stand tall for the Lord as the trees in Heaven do. Time is short and one more soul in Hell is one too many. As Christians we must bring everyone to Christ.

Find a Bible-grace believing church, one that preaches grace through the cleansing blood of Jesus, and remember, you are a part of the Church family. You do not need a church building to give your heart to Jesus, but also please don't forsake gathering with other Christian souls—no matter where that is. Speak to anyone who will listen and make sure they understand that *no* choice *is* a choice, and that they are destined for Hell.

Satan is watching you and hoping you do not accept Jesus. Jesus and the Father are watching and waiting with open arms for you to accept Jesus as your Savior. You have a choice and only you can make it.

Some people may say that the experience I had did not really happen, that it was the hospital drugs, my brain's imagination, or a dream state, but if that is true, let me ask you this, how did I talk with so many people I knew?

Better yet, how did I talk to people I did not know that gave me messages which proved to be true for so many?

Others have asked if I recognize anyone in Hell. I can only say no one could recognize but, I can say this I did not see any children or any type of animals anywhere in Hell. I didn't see any children arriving into Hell through the vortex. I contributed that to "the age of accountability".

Like everything else you must make a choice. You must answer for yourself a few questions: Is this true or not? Does Jesus really exist? Is there really a heaven and a hell? You cannot believe there is one without the other. Just being a good person and doing good things all though admirable will not get you into heaven.

"For by grace you have been saved through faith, and that not of yourselves; it is the gift of God, not of works, lest anyone should boast" (Ephesians 2:8-9, NKJV).

You must accept Jesus as your savior it is the only way.

"God made him who had no sin to be sin for us, so that in him we might become the righteousness of God" (2 Corinthians 5:21, NIV).

Since I have recovered from the experience, I now have a totally new respect for water. I cannot get enough of it. While I was recovering from the surgery, I told everyone when I returned home the first thing I wanted was a tall ice-cold glass of water with lots of ice, not in a plastic cup, but a real chilled cup made of glass. And I did as soon as I returned home. Also, food was like I was tasting it for the first time. It was amazing.

I am doing much better today with the LVAD and feel better than I have in years. The way things have changed since my return home has been amazing. We see Gods Blessings everywhere in our lives. I give all the praise and Glory to God.

No matter what you are going through in life, or how bad things seem to get, if you believe in Jesus and leave it in his hand's things will get better.

I still see glimpses of Satan's creatures now and again, and I know they are here doing Satan's work, but I just keep pushing forward.

If you want to accept Jesus as your savior and have eternal life in Heaven, simply pray this prayer.

> *Lord Jesus, for too long I have kept you out of my life. I know I am a sinner and that I cannot save myself. No longer will I close the door when I hear you knocking. By faith I gratefully receive your gift of salvation. I am ready to trust you as my Lord and Savior. Thank you, Lord Jesus, for coming to earth. I believe you are the Son of God who died on the cross for my sins and rose from the dead on the third day. Thank you for bearing my sins and giving me the gift of eternal life. I believe your words are true. I believe in my heart and confess with my mouth that Jesus is my Lord and Savior. Amen.*

If you have prayed this prayer in sincere faith, place your name or initials by the prayer along with today's date as a reminder that you have come to Christ in faith today, that you trust him as your Lord and Savior. I will see you in Heaven one day. And, believe me, what a glorious place it is!

Just a side note, sometimes we don't understand how we affect other people's lives, because of Bob and Peggy, our walk grew with the Lord. We paid it forward to Alice and her sister Jess, whom we love dearly, with their walk with the Lord. What you do and say for the Lord sometimes seems to fall on deaf ears, but you have no idea how that has affected someone and how it continues to be passed forward to others.

May God Bless you!

Printed in Great Britain
by Amazon

30966423R00069